CCPs provide long-term guidance for management decisions and set forth goals, objectives, and strategies needed to accomplish refuge purposes and identify the Service's best estimate of future needs. These plans detail program planning levels that are sometimes substantially above current budget allocations and, as such, are primarily for Service strategic planning and program prioritization purposes. The plans do not constitute a commitment for staffing increases, operational and maintenance increases, or funding for future land acquisition.

WAUBAY NATIONAL WILDLIFE REFUGE COMPLEX

including
Waubay National Wildlife Refuge
and
Waubay Wetland Management District

COMPREHENSIVE CONSERVATION PLAN

September 2002

Prepared by U.S. Fish & Wildlife Service

Waubay National Wildlife Refuge Complex
44401 134A Street
Waubay, South Dakota 57273-5301

and

Division of Planning
Region 6, Mountain-Prairie Region
P.O. Box 25486, DFC
Denver, Colorado 80225-0486

Approved: _____   8/30/02
ACTING   Regional Director, Region 6, Denver, Colorado   Date

**Waubay National Wildlife Refuge Complex
Comprehensive Conservation Plan Approval
U.S. Fish and Wildlife Service, Region 6**

Submitted By:

_____   _23 aug. 2002_
Larry D. Martin   Date
Project Leader
Waubay National Wildlife Refuge Complex

Concur:

_____   _5/29/02_
Ron Shupe   Date
Refuge Program Supervisor

_____   _8/30/02_
Richard A. Coleman, PhD   Date
Regional Chief
National Wildlife Refuge System

Summary

Waubay National Wildlife Refuge (Refuge), comprised of 4,650 acres, is located in Day County in northeastern South Dakota (Map 1). The Refuge's mix of lakes, wetlands, prairie, forests, and cropland is home to a diversity of wildlife. More than 100 bird species nest on this small piece of habitat, with 37 mammals also calling it home. Waubay National Wildlife Refuge (NWR) was established by President Roosevelt in 1935 as "a refuge and breeding ground for migratory birds and other wildlife."

Waubay Wetland Management District (WMD) protects over 250,000 acres of wetlands and prairie in six counties of northeastern South Dakota. The area's mix of native grass, planted grasses, cropland, and wetlands support a variety of wildlife. Wildlife communities are dependent on the abundant grasslands or wetlands, or both. The WMD is home to 247 species of birds, 43 species of mammals, and over 20 species of amphibians and reptiles. Breeding waterfowl and grassland-dependent passerines are two groups that are especially prominent.

Comprehensive planning is being undertaken for the Refuge and the Wetland Management District (Complex) to guide management for the next 15 years. When completed, the Comprehensive Conservation Plan (CCP) will provide clear goals and objectives, implementation strategies, and recommended staffing and funding for the Complex. This Plan will meet the planning requirements of the National Wildlife Refuge Improvement Act of 1997.

The main goals set forth in the CCP for the Waubay Complex are:

- **Habitat Goal:** *To preserve, restore and enhance the ecological diversity of grasslands, wetlands, and native woodlands of the Prairie Pothole Region of the Great Plains on Waubay National Wildlife Refuge Complex.*

- **Wildlife Goal:** *To promote a natural diversity and abundance of native flora and fauna of the Prairie Pothole Region of the Great Plains on Waubay National Wildlife Refuge Complex.*

- **Cultural Resources Goal:** *Protect and interpret significant historic and prehistoric cultural resources associated with Waubay National Wildlife Refuge Complex.*

- **Wildlife-dependent Recreation Goal:** *To foster an understanding and appreciation of the ecology and management of the fauna and flora and of the role of humans in the Prairie Pothole Region of the Great Plains by providing Complex visitors of all abilities with compatible wildlife-dependent recreational experiences.*

These goals will help fulfill the mission and goals of the U.S. Fish & Wildlife Service and the National Wildlife Refuge System. In an ecosystem setting, Waubay Complex CCP actions will also help meet the goals of the North American Waterfowl Management Plan, Partners in Flight, The Nature Conservancy's Tallgrass Prairie Ecoregional Plan and others. Only by working together can we improve the biological, social, and economic status of the northeastern corner of South Dakota and the Great Plains.

> *"Like wind and sunsets, wild things were taken for granted until progress began to do away with them. Now we face the question whether a still higher 'standard of living' is worth its cost in things natural, wild and free. For us of the minority, the opportunity to see geese is more important than television, and the chance to find a pasque-flower is a right as inalienable as free speech."*
> Aldo Leopold

The National Environmental Policy Act (NEPA) of 1969 stipulates that a written assessment must be made of any action proposed by an agency of the Federal Government that significantly affects the quality of the human environment or has significant impacts on the affected State or Federal land. NEPA also requires Federal decision makers to study, develop, and describe appropriate alternatives to the recommended action. Views of other Federal and State agencies and the public are solicited during the decision making process. An Environmental Assessment (EA) was prepared to accompany the Draft CCP. The proposed action was to prepare and implement the CCP, or enhanced management alternative.

Table of Contents

V. Implementation and Monitoring

Environmental Action Statement

Finding of No Significant Impact

List of Figures

List of Maps

Appendices

I. Introduction/Background

Comprehensive Conservation Plans

The National Wildlife Refuge System Improvement Act (Refuge Improvement Act), an amendment to the National Wildlife Refuge Administration Act of 1966, was passed by Congress in October of 1997. This historic "organic act," the first in the National Wildlife Refuge System's history, required that Comprehensive Conservation Plans (CCPs) be prepared for all refuges within 15 years. Lands covered by this Act include National Wildlife Refuges and Wetland Management Districts, including grassland, wetland, and conservation easements. The Refuge Improvement Act also clarified compatibility and public use issues on Refuge System lands.

The U.S. Fish & Wildlife Service (Service) worked with Congress to craft the Refuge Improvement Act and supported the planning requirement. This planning effort will assist each station, and the entire National Wildlife Refuge System, to meet the changing needs of wildlife and the public. Public input during the CCP process will provide opportunities to consult with neighbors, customers, and other agencies to ensure that plans are relevant and address natural resource issues and public interests. The Draft CCP discussed the planning process, Waubay Complex's characteristics, and the direction management will take in the next 15 years on Waubay Complex.

Waubay National Wildlife Refuge History

Waubay National Wildlife Refuge was established on December 10, 1935, by Executive Order 7245 "as a refuge and breeding ground for migratory birds and other wildlife." Originally known as "Waubay Bluebill Refuge," it consists of 4,650 acres and was purchased from private landowners through 16 different purchase agreements. At the time of purchase, the upland and water acres were 2,587 and 2,063, respectively. The total cost of acquisition was $62,788.97. Approximately 2,402 acres of meandered lakes were withdrawn from public domain and 2,249 acres were purchased; furthermore, the acres were purchased for about $27.92/acre.

In the "Dust Bowl" days of the 1930s, the Refuge lakes were almost entirely dry, contributing to record low waterfowl populations. Water levels and duck populations gradually rose to an "acceptable" or normal level and remained relatively static until the 1990s (Map 2). Heavy precipitation between 1993 and 1999 caused lake levels to rise more than 15 feet to all-time recorded highs, flooding 100-year-old trees (Map 3). In 1995, when Waubay Lake spilled into Hillebrand's Lake, a sport fishery developed for the first time on the Refuge. Currently perch, northern pike, and walleye populations thrive in Refuge waters. With such drastic water fluctuations came changes in bird species, numbers, and habitats. Today, wood ducks, double-crested cormorants, and great-blue herons thrive on the flooded, wooded islands of the Refuge, while over-water nesting species have virtually disappeared along with the emergent cover.

Time Line/Significant Dates of Waubay NWR

1935 - Waubay Refuge established.
1936 - First manager, Watson E. Beed, reported for duty.
1937 - Refuge land acquisition completed.
    - Waubay giant Canada goose flock started with 30 donated captive geese.
    - Refuge observation tower built.
1938 - Famous wildlife artist Frances Lee Jaques, standing on the shore of Spring Lake with Watson Beed, called Waubay "the perfect refuge."
1942 - Highest number of pheasants recorded on the Refuge - over 10,000.
1947 - Deer hunting allowed for the first time.
1948 - "By this time, the Refuge was the only place in the area where prairie chickens could be found." Prairie chickens soon disappeared from the Refuge.
1957 - Five pair of Cotournix quail released on the Refuge - failed.
1959 - Annual Refuge deer hunts began.
1960 - Nature trail established.
1963 - Twenty-five Rio Grande turkeys released on the Refuge - all disappeared by 1964.
1966 - User fees were charged for the picnic area; use dropped by 50 percent - user fees discontinued after one year.
1973 - Activities within the State of South Dakota and administration of Waubay NWR transferred from Region 3 to Region 6 with an Area Office established in Pierre.
1986 - New Refuge headquarters office built.
1993 - Waubay and Refuge lakes, Spring and Hillebrand's, begin to rise because of heavy precipitation.
1995 - Waubay and Hillebrand's Lakes equalize.
1996 - Refuge east entrance road raised four feet.
1997 - Winter of 1996-1997 totals 80.2 inches of snow (average is 30 to 35 inches).
    - Waubay/Hillebrand's Lakes equalize with Spring Lake.
    - Refuge east entrance road raised 3.3 feet.
1998 - Refuge east entrance road raised 7 feet.
    - Refuge opened to ice fishing only.

Waubay Wetland Management District History

Waubay Wetland Management District (WMD) is one of 37 WMD's throughout the prairie pothole region. They were started as part of the Small Wetlands Acquisition Program (SWAP) in the 1950s to save wetlands from various threats, particularly draining. The passage of Public Law 85-585 in August of 1958, amended the Migratory Bird Hunting and Conservation Stamp Act (Duck Stamp Act) of 1934, allowing for the acquisition of "Waterfowl Production Areas"(WPAs) and "Easements for Waterfowl Management Rights" (easements). The nation's first WPA was acquired within the Waubay study area (now known as the WMD), when the 160-acre McCarlson WPA in Day County was purchased from Arnold McCarlson on January 19, 1959.

The Wetlands Loan Act (P.L. 87-383) was passed on October 4, 1961, and allowed for the advancement of funds against future revenues from Duck Stamp sales. As a result, WMDs were created in 1962. In 1966, Waubay WMD consisted of 10 counties: Brookings, Clark, Codington, Day, Deuel, Grant, Hamlin, Kingsbury, Marshall, and Roberts. In 1970, Brookings, Deuel, Hamlin, and Kingsbury counties were transferred to Madison WMD, leaving the remaining six which make up Waubay WMD today. The grassland easement acquisition program was started in 1989 to help protect upland habitat to compliment the wetland easement program. Waubay is currently the nation's second largest WMD with over 250,000 acres of waterfowl habitat being protected through easements and fee-title lands. Protected areas under fee-title total 39,885 acres, while wetland and grassland easements protect approximately 105,000 and 126,000 acres, respectively. An additional 5,260 acres are protected under conservation easements.

Like Waubay NWR, the WMD has varying wetland and upland habitat types and needs to be managed to benefit waterfowl and other wildlife, as well as human users. Today, prescribed burning has taken the place of prairie wildfires and is one tool used to rejuvenate grasslands. Although prescribed burning has proven effective, constraints such as time, money, and staff limit its use in the past. With additional staff and funding, prescribed burning will be used more extensively as a management tool. Another tool available is haying, but it also has limiting factors. Haying is allowed on fee-title lands by permit only; furthermore, it can only be accomplished after July 15 to protect nesting birds. This deters some producers, because the quality of forage may be reduced. Grassland manipulation within Waubay WMD is primarily accomplished through livestock grazing. This method is most closely related to the natural way of managing grasses with livestock replacing the bison of the past.

Recently, increased precipitation has benefitted the WMD and waterfowl populations dependent on these lands. In 1999, statewide wetland counts exceeded one million for the first time and increased 104 percent above the 10-year and long-term averages. Breeding mallards in South Dakota for 1999 exceeded 3 million for only the third time in history (USFWS 1999).

Time Line/Significant Dates of Waubay WMD

1959 - McCarlson WPA, the nation's first WPA, purchased in Day County.
1961 - Wetland easement program began.
1963 - Wetland Management Office established in Webster; first manager - James Pullium.
1964 - Wetland Management Office closes and function taken over by the Refuge.
1968 - Pheasant restoration program on WPAs started under Karl Mundt funding.
1973 - Activities within the State of South Dakota and administration of Waubay NWR transferred from Region 3 to Region 6 with an Area Office established in Pierre.
1989 - Grassland easement program began.
1994 - Hundreds of township, county, and state roads across the WMD flood from rising waters of wetlands and lakes.

Purpose of and Need for Comprehensive Conservation Plan

Waubay Complex was established to provide "... a refuge and breeding ground for migratory birds and other wildlife." The purpose of the CCP is to accomplish the goals established for the Complex, including:

- Habitat Goal: *To preserve, restore and enhance the ecological diversity of grasslands, wetlands, and native woodlands of the Prairie Pothole Region of the Great Plains on Waubay National Wildlife Refuge Complex.*

- Wildlife Goal: *To promote a natural diversity and abundance of native flora and fauna of the Prairie Pothole Region of the Great Plains on Waubay National Wildlife Refuge Complex.*

- Cultural Resources Goal: *Protect and interpret significant historic and prehistoric cultural resources associated with Waubay National Wildlife Refuge Complex.*

- Wildlife-dependent Recreation Goal: *To foster an understanding and appreciation of the ecology and management of the fauna and flora and of the role of humans in the Prairie Pothole Region of the Great Plains by providing Complex visitors of all abilities with compatible wildlife-dependent recreational experiences.*

The CCP, with its clear management direction laid out in specific objectives and strategies, is needed for several reasons. Since the establishment of the Refuge in 1935 and the WMD in the 1960s, many changes have occurred to the landscape. Much habitat has been lost to agriculture, roads, towns, and other development. This loss of habitat has had a profound effect on wildlife populations that once depended on vast expanses of undisturbed grasslands and wetlands. Management of the Complex as outlined in the CCP will help to stem these losses and help to restore biodiversity to the landscape.

The CCP also addresses the need to provide an understanding and appreciation of wildlife and of people's role in the environment. Providing more environmental programs and better interpretation will increase the public's knowledge about the biological values that continue to be lost each day and the need to prevent further losses. The Plan also calls for increased opportunities for wildlife-compatible recreation.

It is the Service's job to protect and provide habitat for migratory birds and other wildlife - this is our purpose and reason for being. We must do this in a vastly changed landscape, balancing the effects of saving wildlife with economic realities and human needs. By preparing this CCP, documenting our goals and objectives, and involving our partners and the public in the process, we can all gain a better understanding of the issues - from all sides. It doesn't have to be wildlife versus people because all will benefit, economically and personally, from a healthy environment. This CCP will help explain how Waubay Complex fits into the landscape and our role in protecting our natural resources for present and future generations.

National Wildlife Refuge System Mission and Goals

The U.S. Fish & Wildlife Service, which administers the Refuge System, is the only agency of the U.S. government whose primary responsibility is fish, wildlife, and plant conservation. The National Wildlife Refuge System (System) is the world's largest and most diverse collection of lands set aside specifically for wildlife. The Mission of the Refuge System is, *"To administer a national network of lands and waters for the conservation, management, and where appropriate, restoration of the fish, wildlife, and plant resources and their habitats within the United States for the benefit of present and future generations of Americans."* Goals of the System are aimed at fulfilling this mission. Some major goals are to provide for specific classes of wildlife species for which the Federal government is ultimately responsible. These "trust resources" are defined by the purpose of the Refuge and include threatened and endangered species, migratory birds, and anadromous fish. Most refuges provide breeding, migration, or wintering habitat for these species. Nearly all refuges also supply habitat for big game species and resident or nonmigratory wildlife as well.

> *"When one tugs at a single thing in nature, he finds it attached to the rest of the world"* John Muir

Goals of the National Wildlife Refuge System are:
  a. *To fulfill our statutory duty to achieve refuge purpose(s) and further the System mission.*
  b. *Conserve, restore where appropriate, and enhance all species of fish, wildlife, and plants that are endangered or threatened with becoming endangered.*
  c. *Perpetuate migratory bird, interjurisdictional fish, and marine mammal populations.*
  d. *Conserve a diversity of fish, wildlife, and plants.*
  e. *Conserve and restore, where appropriate, representative ecosystems of the United States, including the ecological processes characteristic of those ecosystems.*
  f. *To foster understanding and instill appreciation of fish, wildlife, and plants, and their conservation, by providing the public with safe, high-quality, and compatible wildlife-dependent public use. Such use includes hunting, fishing, wildlife observation and photography, and environmental education and interpretation.*

Individual refuges provide specific requirements for the preservation of trust resources. For example, waterfowl breeding refuges in South and North Dakota provide important wetland and grassland habitats to support populations of waterfowl as required by the Migratory Bird Treaty Act and the North American Waterfowl Management Plan. Waubay Complex supports breeding populations as well as providing migration habitat during spring and fall periods. Sabine NWR, and other refuges in Louisiana and Texas, provide wintering habitat for these populations. The network of lands is critical to these birds* survival; any deficiency in one location will affect the species and the entire network's ability to maintain adequate populations. Other refuges may provide habitat for endangered plants or animals that exist in unique habitats found only in very few locations. Refuges in these situations ensure that populations are protected and habitat is suitable for their use. Refuges, by providing a broad network of lands throughout the United States, help prevent species from being listed as endangered by providing secure habitat for their use and opportunities for recovery.

Under the National Wildlife Refuge System Improvement Act of 1997, six wildlife-dependent recreational uses are recognized as priority public uses of refuge lands. These are hunting, fishing, wildlife observation, wildlife photography, environmental education and interpretation. These and other uses are allowed on refuges only after finding that they are compatible with the purpose of the refuge. Uses are allowed through a special regulation process, individual special use permits, and sometimes through State fishing and hunting regulations.

Waubay National Wildlife Refuge Complex Purpose

Waubay NWR Purpose

". . . as a refuge and breeding ground for migratory birds and other wildlife . . ." Executive Order 7245, dated December 10, 1935. Later Executive Orders allowed for expansion of the Refuge under the same purpose.

Waterfowl Production Area Purpose

". . . as Waterfowl Production Areas" subject to ". . . all of the provisions of such Act [Migratory Bird Conservation Act] . . . except the inviolate sanctuary provisions . . ." 16 U.S.C. 718 § (Migratory Bird Hunting and Conservation Stamp Act)

". . . for any other management purpose, for migratory birds." 16 U.S.C. § 715d (Migratory Bird Conservation Act)

". . . for conservation purposes . . ." 7 U.S.C. § 2002 (Consolidated Farm and Rural Development Act)

Waubay Complex Vision Statement

A vast landscape of native prairie splashed with sparkling blue jewels of pristine wetlands with its variety of wildlife, where people can learn about the unique features and enjoy the bounty of the Coteau des Prairie region.

Although this vision has a dreamlike feel to it, it is founded in a real need to restore the health of the Northern Great Plains. Restoring grasslands and wetlands and protecting and promoting their long-term health will be good not only for wildlife, but for humans as well. The economic health of this region may also soon depend on the soundness of these natural systems as farming becomes economically challenging and more and more people turn to tourism and the fishing/hunting industry to make a living. Already this is becoming a reality with the increased fishing opportunities available with the onset of new and expanded lakes and wetlands. More and more people are also filling their leisure time with outdoor activities such as bird-watching, hiking, or fishing. By restoring and enhancing native habitats, Waubay Complex can help attract visitors providing additional economic opportunities in the area.

Legal and Policy Guidance

The National Wildlife Refuge System started nearly 100 years ago with an Executive Order, signed by President Theodore Roosevelt, protecting a small and unpretentious island full of pelicans, ibises, and spoonbills from market hunters. It wasn't until 1997 that the National Wildlife Refuge System Improvement Act was passed which set the mission and administrative policy for all refuges in the System. It also outlined the importance of the six priority public uses (hunting, fishing, wildlife observation, wildlife photography, environmental education and interpretation) and how they should be promoted except where incompatible with the purpose of the individual Refuge or the system as a whole. A formal process for determining compatibility was also established with this Act. From the first act to the most recent, the overriding principle that guides the Refuge system is wildlife comes first.

Other key legislative policies that direct management of Refuges include the Endangered Species Act (1973), Clean Water Act (1977), Land and Water Conservation Fund Act (1965), Migratory Bird Treaty Act (1918), and Executive Order 12996 Management and General Public Use of the National Wildlife Refuge System (1996). These and other Acts and Executive Orders that guide Refuge System activities are listed in Appendix F. The U.S. Fish & Wildlife Service also provides its own policy guidelines which can be found in Refuge Manuals.

Existing Partnerships

Waubay Complex staff work with a variety of individuals and organizations to accomplish habitat management, outreach, and environmental education projects. Some past and current partners include Sisseton-Wahpeton Sioux Tribe; Ducks Unlimited; County Conservation Districts; South Dakota Game, Fish and Parks; The Nature Conservancy; Ne-So-Dak (Glacial Lakes Outdoor School); local Boy and Girl Scout troops; and numerous private landowners. Far less would be accomplished within and beyond our borders without these partnerships. A complete listing of partners is included in Appendix K.

II. Planning Process

Planning Process, Planning Time Frame, and Future Revisions

Comprehensive Conservation Plans (CCPs) provide a clear and comprehensive statement of desired future conditions for each refuge or planning unit. The CCP will provide long-range guidance and management direction to achieve refuge purposes, help fulfill the Refuge System mission, and maintain or restore the ecological integrity of each Refuge and the System. Additional goals of the CCP process include using science and sound professional judgment to support management decisions, ensuring the six priority public uses receive consideration during the preparation of the CCP, providing a public forum for stakeholders and interested parties to have input in refuge management decisions, and to provide a uniform basis for funding.

The CCP planning process consists of the following eight steps. Although the steps are listed sequentially, CCP planning and National Environmental Policy Act (NEPA) documentation can be iterative. Some of the steps may be repeated or more than one step can occur at the same time.

- ✓ Preplanning - form core team, identify needs
- ✓ Identify Issues and develop Vision - **Public Input Gathered on Issues**
- ✓ Develop Goals and Objectives - from issues, resource relationships, legal responsibilities
- ✓ Develop and Analyze Alternatives, including the Proposed Action
- ✓ Prepare Draft Plan and NEPA Document - assess environmental effects, **Public Comments on Draft Plan Gathered**
- ✓ Prepare and Adopt Final Plan
- ✓ Implement Plan, Monitor and Evaluate
- ✓ Review and Revise Plan

Comprehensive conservation planning efforts for Waubay Complex began in December 1997 with a meeting of regional management and planning staff and field station employees from Waubay Complex and Tewaukon Complex at Tewaukon's headquarters in North Dakota. At that meeting a core planning team was designated with the major responsibilities of gathering information, soliciting public input, and writing the Plan.

Beginning in January of 1998, an extensive scoping effort was undertaken to solicit comments from interested parties. Comments were solicited from at least 29 public gatherings, including open houses, county commissioner meetings, sports/farm shows, sportsman groups, agency meetings, live radio interviews, and other community organizations. Sixteen hundred leaflets were mailed out and media releases also encouraged the public to comment and get involved in the CCP process. Participants were provided an opportunity to learn about the Service and Complex's purposes, mission, goals, and management issues. Everyone had the chance to speak with Service representatives and to share their comments. The mailing list is included in Appendix G.

The CCP will guide management on the Refuge and WMD for the next 15 years. Plans are signed by the Regional Director, Region 6, thus providing Regional direction to the station project leader and staff. Copies of the Plan will be provided to all interested parties when requested. Whenever there is a significant need or at least every 5 years, the project leader will review the Plan and decide if a revision is necessary.

Planning Issues

For the planning team, the biggest issue was the loss and degradation of grassland and wetland habitats. Protecting and restoring these habitats would reduce the continued loss of biodiversity and help restore wildlife populations. Staff felt the best way to accomplish this would be through partnerships, easement acquisition, and improved management of fee-title lands. Habitat fragments would also be reduced by removing food plots, replanting woodlands, and removing or controlling nonnative plants, shrubs, or trees.

Public comments also expressed a need to protect and enhance native habitats. Some were in favor of increased acquisition (fee and easement), but others were not. Many comments encouraged the use and management of native plants and animals and biological control methods for weed control.

Wildlife issues for the planning team centered on increasing baseline data for individual WPAs and developing monitoring and inventory plans. These plans would improve our ability to track management activities and their effects on the landscape and wildlife populations. For the public, comments ranged from wanting more nesting structures to reintroducing elk.

Only a few comments were received during scoping meetings regarding hunting. One was to restrict hunting seasons to only primitive weapons, another to decrease the number of tags offered, and a third to expand youth hunting and fishing programs. Allowing all three deer hunting seasons to continue provides more opportunities for hunters as well as accomplishing Refuge objectives to control deer numbers and protect habitat. Hunting success for muzzleloader and archery seasons is usually about 25 to 30 percent while it is closer to 50 percent or higher for rifle seasons (Refuge files, SDGFP 2001). Providing hunts for youth or people with disabilities will be considered and developed if practicable.

Both the public and the planning team expressed an interest in increasing public use, environmental education, and interpretation. There was also a desire to build better relations with the community and provide more volunteer opportunities. There was a particular interest in increasing the access and availability of fishing on the Refuge. The planning team had to consider the requirements of trust resources, particularly waterfowl, and compatibility issues when addressing these requests. There are also safety and accessibility concerns that need to be considered, as well as the need for additional funding to address these concerns. Issues such as providing additional boat access and stocking fish off-refuge are the primary responsibility of the South Dakota Game, Fish and Parks or other agencies.

The Sisseton-Wahpeton Tribe brought up two issues, bison grazing and collecting plants on Service owned lands within the Complex.

Many of the issues brought up by the public were considered and incorporated into the CCP, but some were dismissed due to incompatibility or other negative impacts. For example, although elk at one time roamed the Great Plains, this issue was not considered due to economic and other constraints.

III. Summary Waubay Complex and Resource Descriptions

Geographic / Ecosystem Setting

Waubay WMD is situated in the northeastern corner of South Dakota, covering Marshall, Roberts, Day, Grant, Clark, and Codington counties. It is comprised of 40,000 acres of Waterfowl Production Areas (WPAs), 105,000 acres of wetland easements, 126,000 acres of grassland easements, and 5,260 acres of Farmer's Home Administration (FmHA) conservation easements. Waubay NWR is located in northeastern Day County and is comprised of 4,650 acres.

Northeastern South Dakota is within the Central Lowlands Province, a major physiographic province (Westin and Malo 1978). Prairie potholes, the major land feature, were formed between 12,000 and 40,000 years ago during Pleistocene glaciations. The first ice sheet covering eastern South Dakota was the Nebraskan, followed by the Kansan, Illinoisan, and Wisconsin ice sheets. The Wisconsin ice sheet had four separate advances. Four distinct physiographic regions cover Waubay Complex from east to west: Minnesota River-Red River Lowlands, Coteau Des Prairies, Lake Dakota Plain, and the James River Lowland (Map 4).

Figure 1. Prairie Pothole Region

The Minnesota River-Red River Lowland was formed from sediment deposited on the bottom of ancient Glacial Lake Agassiz. Drainage runs north into the Red River of the North or south into the Minnesota River along the Continental Divide. This Divide, unlike the one located in the Rockies, separates the continent depending on whether water flows north to Hudson Bay or south to the Gulf of Mexico. The Coteau des Prairies is a series of north-south parallel moraines which rise 800 feet or more in elevation above adjacent lowlands. Numerous wetland basins are a prominent feature of this land form. About 80 percent of Waubay Complex is situated within the Coteau des Prairies. The Lake Dakota Plain was formed from silt and sand deposits under old Lake Dakota. Flowing water drains into the James River. The James River Lowland is a large glacially-eroded valley drained by the James River.

Waubay Complex is located wholly within the Prairie Pothole Region of the Upper Great Plains (Figure 1). It is also part of the Prairie Pothole Joint Venture area, a geographic region of importance to the North American Waterfowl Management Plan. The prairie pothole wetland complexes and associated grasslands are an integral component of the prairie landscape, providing a wide array of ecological, social, and economic benefits. A high density of wetlands in this region helps produce the majority of game ducks, yet contains only 10 percent of the breeding habitat in the continent (Baldassarre and Bolen 1994).

There are four flyways denoting major migration pathways that funnel waterfowl from wintering to breeding habitat and back. Continental waterfowl management today is based on this flyway concept. Waubay Complex is on the eastern edge of the Central Flyway.

Waubay Complex falls under the jurisdiction of Region 6 of the U.S. Fish & Wildlife Service and is part of the Mainstem Missouri River ecosystem (Map 5). Goals and objectives for this Ecosystem can be found in Appendix I.

Waubay Complex also falls within the bounds of numerous other ecosystems and other planning efforts such as The Nature Conservancy's Ecoregional Plan for the Tallgrass Prairie, North American Waterfowl Management Plan and the Prairie Pothole Joint Venture, Partners in Flight, and the South Dakota Natural Heritage Program. A brief listing of these and other programs or planning efforts that affect Waubay Complex is listed in Appendix M.

The Sisseton-Wahpeton Sioux Tribe owns thousands of acres within Lake Traverse Reservation. The Reservation, created by treaty in 1867, covers portions of five northeastern counties in South Dakota and two southeastern counties in North Dakota. Much of the land within the reservation was opened up to Euro-American settlement in 1892. Native American landownership within the reservation then took on two forms: tribal land and heirship trust land, the latter owned by the descendants of male tribal members who had received allotments of land in 1892. Heirship trust land is managed for the owners by the Bureau of Indian Affairs.

Historically, the landscape of northeastern South Dakota consisted of a vast expanse of tall and mixed grass prairie with numerous shallow and deep wetlands. Woodlands would have developed and been protected from prairie fires around larger lakes and in the cooler, moister coulees coming off of the Coteau. No nonnative plants would have been present. A rich assortment of native plants and wildlife existed, evolved with, and were maintained by fire, periodic defoliation by large herds of grazing animals, and climate.

As European settlement of the Northern Great Plains progressed, many changes occurred on the land. Two of the processes which shaped grassland communities were suppressed or eliminated (fire and herds of bison and elk) and settlers began planting shelterbelts and woodlands to control soil and wind erosion. Agriculture soon dominated the landscape and lifestyles of the inhabitants in the early-to-mid-1900s. Nonnative grasses were planted for pastures and hay, while large portions of native prairie were plowed up for cropland. Wetlands were drained to provide more cropland and make farming operations easier and more profitable. The vast prairie that once existed was soon covered by roads, railroads, houses, towns, trees, noxious weeds, and nonnative grasses.

Climate

The climate is typically continental, characterized by cold winters and hot summers. Winter and summer temperatures can vary from extremes of -43°F to 104°F. More common temperatures range from -26°F to 95°F. Average annual precipitation is 20.9 inches and is normally heaviest in late spring and early summer. Intense thunderstorms are normal occurrences in summer. Frequent spells of dry years often alternate with years that are wetter than average. Wetland levels can fluctuate widely with these precipitation changes. The average seasonal snowfall is 30 to 35 inches. Combined snow and high winds often produce blizzard conditions in the area. Prevailing winds are from the northwest. Wind speeds average 13 miles per hour, but can often be much higher, especially in the spring. The growing season varies from 109 to 112 days.

Waubay NWR has been an official weather station since 1953. Climatological conditions have generally been extremely wet since 1992 (Figure 2). Every year since then has recorded higher than average precipitation. Low evaporation conditions also prevailed throughout this period. This has led to water levels not seen in 200 to 500 years in many closed basins in the WMD. For example, Waubay Lake has risen more then 20 feet in 12 years (Figure 3).

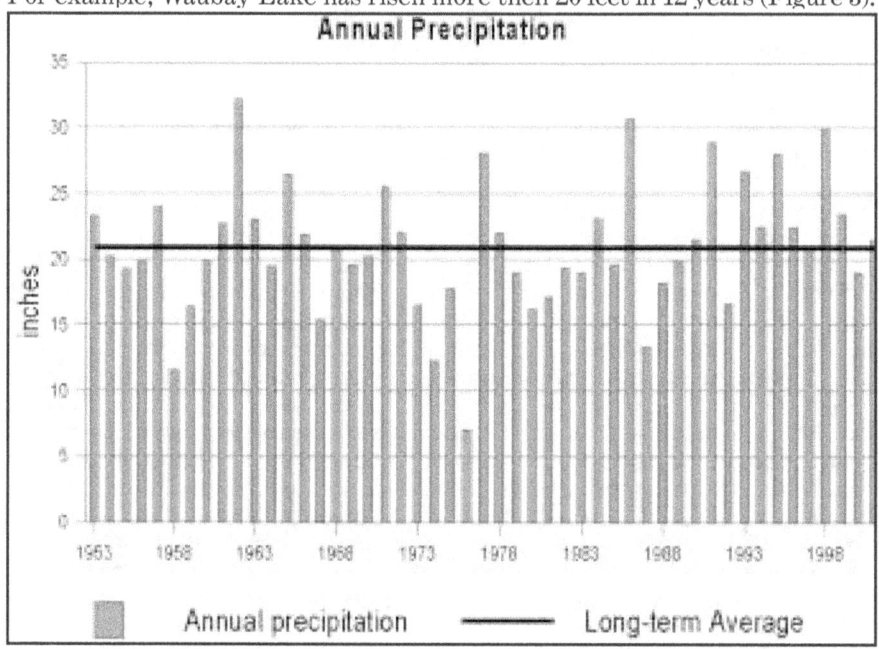

Figure 2. Annual and long-term average precipitation at Waubay NWR, 1953-2001.

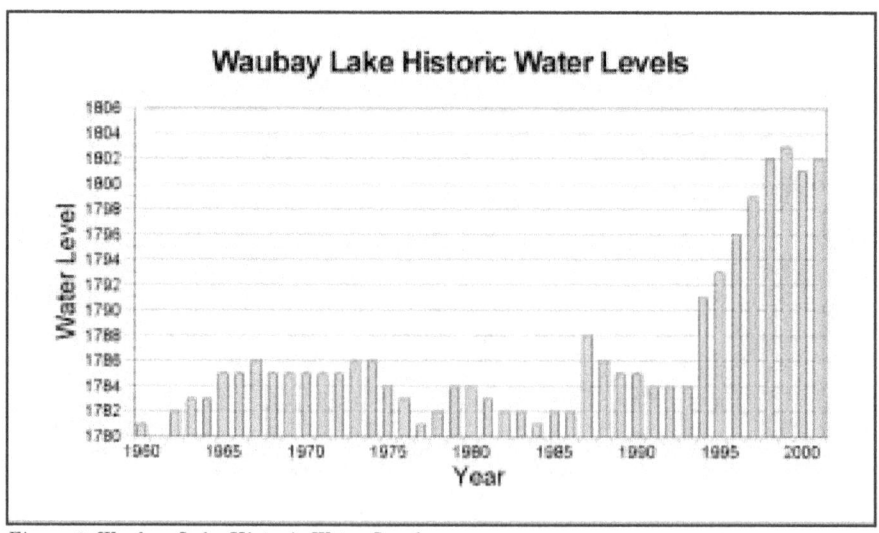

Figure 3. Waubay Lake Historic Water Levels.

Air Quality

Waubay Wetland Management District, encompassing the National Wildlife Refuge, meets attainment status for pollutants as reported by South Dakota Department of Environment and Natural Resources.

Soils

Soils have been inventoried and mapped, and county soil surveys have been published for the Waubay Complex. The soil associations vary greatly according to the physiographic regions. The soils are derived from parent materials which include glaciolacustrine sediments, early Wisconsin glacial drift, and late-Wisconsin glacial drift (loess).

The Coteau des Prairies consists of relief that is undulating to steep. The landscape is characterized by many potholes or depressions. The drainage pattern is poorly defined, except near the Big Sioux River where the level to moderately sloping loamy Brookings-Kranzburg-Vienna soils predominate. Coteau soils consist primarily of the Forman-Aastad-Buse association which are well drained, nearly level to steep loamy soils formed in glacial till. Stones and boulders scattered on the surface in some areas limit the use of these soils for cultivation.

The Lake Dakota Plain extends into the western counties of Marshall and Day and is a plain of lacustrine material. Lacustrine deposits are alternating levels of clay and sandy sediments. The primary soil associations are the Great Bend-Beotia and Harmony-Aberdeen-Nahon associations. Soils are generally silty and moderately well drained, but there are areas with poor drainage.

The James River Lowland consists of level to rolling, loamy soils that are moderately well drained. The principal associations within this region are the Niobell-Noonan-Williams, Barnes-Svea, and Bryant. Drainage systems of these associations are poorly defined, and many terminate to form small basins.

The Minnesota River-Red River Lowland extends into the eastern half of Roberts and Grant counties on a plain of lacustrine silts. Principal associations include Heimdal-Svea-Sisseton, Poinsett-Eckman-Heimdal, and Forman-Aastad. Soils are moderately well drained, nearly level to sloping, and silty or loamy.

Waubay Complex Resources

The Service has management and administrative responsibility on essentially five different types of land holdings. This does not include the Private Lands Program. These land holdings are described as follows:

1. National Wildlife Refuge

Waubay is derived from a Lakota word meaning "a place where numbers of birds make their nests." Waubay National Wildlife Refuge was purchased to further the purposes of the Migratory Bird Conservation Act. It is owned by the Service in fee-title and managed to provide high-quality wetlands and nesting cover primarily for waterfowl and other migratory birds. Many other wildlife species also benefit from the management, including white-tailed deer and ring-necked pheasant. The Refuge is open for deer hunting and ice fishing as well as wildlife observation, wildlife photography, environmental education and interpretation.

The Refuge consists of 4,650 acres. Habitat types are approximately 48 percent grassland, 35 percent wetland, 14 percent woodland/brush, and 3 percent cropland (Map 6). Woodlands are surrounded by large glacial lakes and are thought to have developed because they were protected from prairie wildfires that commonly occurred on surrounding open prairie. Bur oak, basswood, green ash, American elm, hackberry, and cottonwood are the major tree species.

The following types of land holdings are located within the boundaries of the Wetland Management District:

2. Waterfowl Production Areas

Waterfowl Production Areas (WPAs) are lands purchased by the Service under the provisions of the Migratory Bird Hunting and Conservation Stamp Act, as amended in 1958. Funding for these purchases comes from the sale of Migratory Bird Hunting and Conservation Stamps (Federal Duck Stamp). These lands are owned by the Service in fee-title and managed to provide high quality wetlands and nesting cover primarily for waterfowl and other migratory birds. Other wildlife species also benefit from these areas. WPAs are open to the public for hunting, fishing, and trapping. New WPAs are currently purchased only if they are round-outs to existing WPAs or have some special features. On average, a new WPA is purchased every 5 years.

The Service owns and manages a total of 39,885 WPA acres within the WMD (Map 7). There are 199 WPA units which range from 3 acres to over 1,325 acres and may consist of more than one acquisition tract. Habitat types are approximately 56 percent grassland, 40 percent wetland, 0.5 percent cropland, 1.8 percent woodland, and 1.3 percent brush.

3. Wetland Easements

The wetland easement program was authorized by Congress on August 1, 1958, and like WPAs, is financed by receipts from the sale of Federal Duck Stamps. Under this program, willing landowners are paid one lump sum payment to not drain, burn, level, or fill natural wetlands. Wetlands must be of value to waterfowl before they are considered for easement purchase. These easements cover only the wetland acres on the land and are perpetual, that is, they are permanent. Ownership remains with the landowner and the Service acquires no other management rights with the easement. Easements do not affect normal farming practices such as cropping, haying, grazing, plowing, or cultivating wetlands when they are dry due to natural conditions.

The WMD currently protects approximately 105,000 acres of wetlands with waterfowl management easements. Acres of easements change regularly as acquisition is still active. All wetlands under easement are inspected annually by Service personnel for possible violations of the easement contract.

4. Grassland Easements

In 1989, the Service began the grassland easement program to protect important nesting cover and enhance water quality on privately owned lands. Like wetland easements, grassland easements are perpetual, with the Service purchasing certain rights to the grassland acres. Under this program, willing landowners retain ownership and grazing is unrestricted. However, disturbance of the soil, such as in the production of agricultural crops, is prohibited and haying is allowed only after July 15 each year to reduce disturbance to ground-nesting birds. All grassland easement tracts are also covered by wetland easements. Grassland easements are inspected yearly for possible violations of the easement contract.

Each potential easement is evaluated for its value to wildlife. Lands must rate 40 pairs/square mile or higher on the Waterfowl Breeding Pair Distributions (Map 8). Large native grass tracts with good wetland complexes that include brood water are given the highest priority. Tracts must protect at least 160 acres and have perpetually protected brood water within one mile of the tract to be considered for an easement. Easements less than 160 acres must be adjacent to other grassland easements, WPAs, or South Dakota Game, Fish and Parks (SDGFP) lands, to make up 160 acres of protected grasslands. Occasionally, a tract is purchased with a portion of the land still in crop production. The landowner enters into an agreement to seed the cropland back to a recommended grass mixture to qualify for the easement.

Grassland easements within the WMD range in size from approximately 40 to over 2,720 contiguous acres. Currently, approximately 126,000 acres are protected under the grassland easement program. This program is expanding with new easement contracts written every month. The Service acquires no other management rights with the easement document.

The Dakota Tallgrass Prairie Wildlife Management Area (DTP-WMA) is a new Refuge addition intended to eventually preserve 190,000 acres of remaining northern tallgrass prairie in eastern South Dakota and southeastern North Dakota. The DTP-WMA augments the decade old grassland easement program, funded by Migratory Bird Stamps, by purchasing grassland easements in areas in which the Service cannot use Migratory Bird Stamp funding. The DTP-WMA boundary includes over 80 percent of the remaining northern tallgrass prairie. The DTP-WMA includes parts of 4 counties in North Dakota and 28 counties in South Dakota, including all of the counties in the Waubay WMD. Large blocks of prairie of 10,000 - 20,000 acres are the primary targets for enrollment into the program. Preservation of the prairie will mainly be in the form of grassland protection easements. Stipulations and ground disturbing restrictions are the same as on the above stated grassland easements purchased with Migratory Bird Stamp monies. Funding for the DTP-WMA comes directly from Congressional appropriations in the form of Land and Water Conservation Funds (LWCF). The northern tallgrass prairie is the most altered and possibly the most endangered ecosystem in North America. Today, less than 4 percent of the original northern tallgrass prairie remains. This means that almost 45 million acres of northern tallgrass prairie have disappeared, mostly due to continuous conversion of prairie to croplands since the late 1800s. The rich diversity of the northern tallgrass prairie consists of at least 300 species of plants, 113 species of butterflies, 35 reptile and amphibian species, 60 mammal species, and 260 species of birds that are known to breed in or use the area.

5. Farmers Home Administration Conservation Easements

The Federal agency previously called the Farmers Home Administration (FmHA) of the U.S. Department of Agriculture (USDA) is required by Executive Order 11990 to preserve and protect all wetlands that were in FmHA ownership. The 1985 and 1990 Food Security Acts (Farm Bill) gave direction as to how and by whom this should be accomplished. Cooperating with FmHA, the Service would recommend "conservation easements" on FmHA inventory properties. When these properties sold to private ownership, the Service accepted the responsibility of enforcing the terms of the conservation easements. Presently, 5,263 acres of former FmHA inventory properties are under some type of conservation easement. These easements, at a minimum, protect the wetlands from burning, draining, or filling. There are 1,242 acres of wetlands protected. In some cases, the easements protect adjacent upland habitat as well. Some upland easements protect the land from ever being farmed, while others restrict nearly all uses of the land. Due to a change in the way USDA defines wetlands, it is expected that there will be no additional conservation easements.

Water Resources and Associated Wetlands

Wetlands are lands where saturation with water is the dominant factor determining the nature of soil development and the types of plant and animal communities living in the soil and on its surface (Cowardin et al. 1979). It is estimated that the contiguous United States contained 221 million acres of wetlands just 200 years ago (Dahl 1990). By the mid-1970s, only 46 percent of the original acreage remained (Tiner 1984). Wetlands now cover about 5 percent of the landscape of the lower 48 states. Wetlands are extremely productive and important to both migratory and resident wildlife. They serve as breeding and nesting areas for many migratory birds and as wintering habitat for many species of resident wildlife. Humans also benefit from wetlands, which can improve water quality and quantity, reduce flooding effects, and provide sites for recreation. Economically, wetlands provide places to hunt, fish, trap, or bird-watch for millions of Americans. In the 1996 Survey of Fishing, Hunting and Wildlife Associated Recreation, about 40 percent of U.S. residents 16 years or older participated in wildlife related activities. More than $100 billion was spent in pursuit of these activities, most of which depend on productive wetlands (USFWS 1996).

Wetlands can be classified by vegetation, water regimes (the length of time water occupies a specific area), and water chemistry. More specifically, prairie potholes are described using the following nontidal water regime modifiers from Cowardin et al. (1979).

- Temporarily flooded - surface water is present for brief periods during the growing season. The water table usually lies below the soil surface most of the season, so plants that grow in both uplands and wetlands are characteristic.
- Seasonally flooded - surface water is present for extended periods especially early in the growing season, but is absent by the end of the season in most years. When surface water is absent, the water table is often near the surface.
- Semipermanently flooded - surface water persists throughout the growing season in most years. When surface water is absent, the water table is usually at or very near the land surface.
- Permanently flooded - water covers the land throughout the year in all years. Vegetation is composed of obligate hydrophytes, such as cattails.

Even though drainage and other wetland decimating factors have taken their toll, wetlands are still a prominent feature of the Complex's landscape (Map 9). The National Wetland Inventory has identified 348,482 wetland acres in the WMD. These include ponds ranging from 0.1 acre with temporary water regimes to large glacial lakes to major rivers and smaller tributaries.

In the James and Minnesota-Red River lowlands, temporarily and seasonally flooded basins are more predominant while semipermanently and permanently flooded wetlands are most abundant on the Prairie Coteau. The average size of wetlands in eastern South Dakota is only .4 acre; 72.9 percent of wetlands are #1 acre and 92.1 percent are #5 (Johnson and Higgins 1997).

The eastern edge of the WMD is bordered by Big Stone Lake, an impoundment of the Minnesota River, and Lake Traverse, an impoundment of the Red River of the North. The Big Sioux River drains the south-central portion of the WMD and empties into the Missouri River in southeastern South Dakota. The Big Sioux is a typical prairie river, often flooding in spring and drying up in summer. When wet, however, the Big Sioux offers tremendous benefits to many species of wetland-dependent plants and animals.

> "Greater familiarity with marshes on the part of more people could give man a truer and more wholesome view of himself in relation to Nature . . . . Marshes comprise their own form of wilderness. They have their own life-rich genuineness and reflect forces that are much older, much more permanent and much mightier than man."
> Paul Errington

Vegetation
Upland Vegetation

The following native plant communities as developed by The Nature Conservancy (Anderson et al. 1998) and used by State Natural Heritage Programs can be found in the WMD.

Native Prairie

Little Bluestem-Porcupine Grass Dry-Mesic Hill Prairie
Hill prairie is found on moderate to steep slopes with soils that are dry. This community is dominated by grasses such as little bluestem, porcupine grass, sideoats grama, and western wheatgrass. Common forbs include leadplant, rigid goldenrod, purple and prairie coneflowers.

Northern Mesic Tallgrass Prairie
Some of the largest remaining tracts of tallgrass prairie occur in the Prairie Coteau where rolling, rocky topography prevented conversion to cropland. It is found on level to gentle slopes with mesic soils. The prairie is dominated by tall grasses such as big bluestem, along with shorter grasses like northern dropseed and porcupine grass. Common forbs include leadplant, prairie lousewort, and golden alexander.

Northern Wet-Mesic Tallgrass Prairie
This is found in low lying areas and drainage ways, but rarely occupies more than a few acres in size. The water table is often near the surface. It is dominated by big bluestem and Canada bluejoint. Common forbs include Rocky Mountain blazing star.

Forests, Woodlands and Savanna

Northern Bur Oak Mesic Forest
This plant community is found primarily in coulees and adjacent uplands and is more common on the eastern edge of the Coteau. It is mostly found on south or west-facing slopes and with moist soils. The canopy is dominated by bur oak, with smaller amounts of basswood and green ash. Ironwood is a common small tree/subcanopy species. The shrub layer may have American hazelnut, dogwood, gooseberry, prickly ash, rose, and serviceberry. The herb layer has a diversity of species including hog peanut, Pennsylvania sedge, columbine and sweet cicely.

Plains Basswood Forest
This forest type is found primarily on the north or east-facing slopes on moist soils in coulees and adjacent uplands. It is found only on the eastern edge of the Coteau because the coulees on the eastern side are deeper and wider than those on the western side, as well as east or northeast- facing, providing a more suitable microclimate for this forest type. The canopy is dominated by American basswood, with smaller amounts of green ash, bur oak, hackberry, and quaking aspen. Sugar maple can be locally dominant on the northeast portion of the Prairie Coteau, the only place on this land form where it occurs. Ironwood is a common small tree / subcanopy species. The shrub layer may include gooseberry and serviceberry. The herb layer may include Virginia waterleaf, sweet cicely, blue cohosh, bloodroot, and red baneberry. Some of the herbs found here, as well as in the Northern Bur Oak Mesic Forest, are typical eastern deciduous forest species and are on the western edge of their range.

Bur Oak Woodland
This community occurs on dry to mesic sites and is floristically and structurally intermediate between Northern Bur Oak Mesic Forest and Bur Oak Savanna. It has a patchy canopy and an understory dominated by shrubs and tree saplings. The primary species in the canopy is bur oak. The shrub layer can range from scattered to a dense thicket. It may include raspberries, gooseberries, dogwoods, American hazelnut, and prickly ash. Prairie vegetation, if present, only occurs in small openings in the tree or shrub layer. The herbacious layer is generally sparse and floristically poor.

Bur Oak Savanna
This dry to dry-mesic community is dominated by bur oak. The stature and spacing of trees is somewhat variable, reflecting differences in soils, topography, and climate, factors that strongly affect local droughtiness and fire frequency. Shrub cover is variable and consists of oak grubs, American hazelnut, serviceberry, and buckbrush. The herbaceous layer is dominated by species typically found in Little Bluestem-Porcupine Grass Dry-Mesic Hill Prairie. This is a fire maintained community and, due to fire suppression, much of it has probably converted to bur oak woodland or forest.

The 75-acre woodland area north of Hillebrand's Lake is designated by the Society of American Foresters as a Research Natural Area because of its unique bur oak/little bluestem cover type. No special management occurs from this designation.

The six counties of northeastern South Dakota encompass 3.4 million acres, half of which has been converted to cropland (Map 10). Of the 1.3 million acres of remaining grasslands, approximately 1.0 million acres is considered native prairie. This "native" prairie is defined as grassland that has never been plowed, but in reality all plant communities have been altered somewhat from pristine conditions due to exotic plant introductions, livestock grazing impacts, lack of fire, and other factors since European settlement.

Grassland vegetation makes up approximately 54 percent of Service lands within the Complex. On WPAs, approximately 95 percent of uplands consist of grasslands. On the Refuge, 71 percent of uplands are grasslands, with the remainder in trees, brush or developments. Of these grassland acres, approximately 65 percent is native grassland and 35 percent is seeded exotic grass/forb mixes or restored native grasses.

As part of the Northern Great Plains, two major vegetation types are represented within the Complex - tallgrass prairie and northern mixed-grass prairie (Johnson and Larson 1999). The tallgrass, or true prairie, extends along the eastern Dakotas and Nebraska into Minnesota and Iowa. Less than 4 percent of the original tallgrass prairie ecosystem is left and more is lost each year (Steinauer and Collins 1996). All of the Minnesota River-Red River Lowland and much of the Coteau des Prairies lie within this vegetation type. Tallgrass prairie gradually gives way to northern mixed-grass prairie to the west, generally covering the Lake Dakota Plain and James River basin. Remnant stands of eastern deciduous forest grow in ravines and north-facing slopes along the Coteau des Prairies and adjacent to bigger lakes on the Coteau.

In addition to these natural vegetation types, approximately 35 percent of Service lands are covered by planted tame (or exotic) grasses or restored natives. Tame grasslands generally consist of smooth brome or Kentucky bluegrass, and few forbs. Both of these exotic grasses can be found on native prairie tracts, often compromising the health, vigor, and diversity of native sites. Restored native sites generally consist of a mix of four or five grass species such as big and little bluestem, sideoats grama, switchgrass, green needle grass, and a legume such as alfalfa or Canada milkvetch. Currently, no other forbs are used in restoration efforts, mostly due to high costs and difficulty in acquiring seeds suited to this location.

There are two primary ways to evaluate grassland condition. One is range condition, which is based on percentages of selected native plant species present at a given time as compared to percentages present under a climax range condition. The second is forage or vegetative condition, which is more commonly referred to as grassland vigor. This method does not evaluate grasslands based on species composition, but rather health of the plants. In general, both range condition and vegetative condition of WPAs are in fair-to-poor condition.

Wetland Vegetation

Wetland vegetation refers to those plants which grow in water or in soils which are saturated for most of the growing season. Wetland vegetation is broken down into four major categories of plants, based on their growth form and the wetland zone they inhabit. These categories are free-floating, submergent, emergent, and amphibious.

Free-floating are those wetland plants which float at or beneath the surface of the water without attached roots. Common examples are duckweed, bladderwort, and coontail. Submergent plants are those which have roots in the substrate, and do not emerge above the surface of the water, except some may have floating leaves. Examples are pondweed, water milfoil, waterweed, and widgeongrass. Emergent wetland plants are rooted in the substrate and the foliage grows partially or entirely above the water surface. Arrowhead, cattail, common reed, and bulrush are common examples. Amphibious refers to wetland plants that can grow as either a submergent or an emergent. Commonly, water levels drop, leaving these plants growing in a temporarily dry site. Some common plants are yellow water-crowfoot, pepperwort, and water smartweed.

Wetlands cover approximately 40 percent of WPAs and 35 percent of the Refuge. Most of these acres have one or more types of wetland plants. It is not uncommon for a single wetland to have all four categories of aquatic vegetation.

Endangered Plants

The Western prairie fringed orchid is the only known federally threatened plant species that may be present on the Complex. Historical locations have included sites in the Big Sioux River valley in the southeastern part of South Dakota. It occurs in moist, tallgrass prairies and sedge meadows, both of which can be found in the WMD. It appears to have been extirpated from South Dakota, but remote populations may have been overlooked as it does occur in adjacent counties of Minnesota, North Dakota, Iowa, and Nebraska.

The major reason for its decline is the conversion of native prairie habitat into cropland and tame pasture. Heavy grazing, early haying, lack of fire, and noxious weed infestations can all have detrimental effects on this orchid. Widespread use of herbicides can also be a problem. Conversely, using herbicides in localized areas only, can be beneficial by removing competing, nonnative species. Preserves where the Western prairie fringed orchid is currently located are often managed by prescribed burning. Burning is used to reduce mulch buildup and control the increase of nonnative and woody plant species. This species of orchid is well adapted to survive periodic fires. It is not known whether carefully timed short-duration grazing or haying will have similar beneficial effects. Research is continuing in these areas. Moderate uses of these tools may have no effect as orchids have been known to persist on private lands in some grazed prairies and hayland (USFWS 1993; MN Department of Natural Resources 1991).

Noxious Plants

Many noxious plant species exist within the WMD. Most are introduced species with no natural controls. The primary ones on WPAs are Canada thistle, leafy spurge, and wormwood sage. These species often compete with and have a very negative effect on native plant species. The control of noxious plants is important to benefit native plant communities and is required by State law.

Wildlife

Wildlife communities have changed significantly since settlement. Knickerbocker (1869) listed elk, buffalo, antelope, grey wolf, black bear, otter, and marten as occurring in the vicinity of Fort Sisseton, in Marshall County. All have been extirpated from the region. Small herds of antelope have been reintroduced and some buffalo are raised in domestic herds on ranches. The Fort commander issued an order in 1876 prohibiting killing prairie chickens on the military reservation, due to serious reductions in the population. Prairie chicken numbers have been low since the 1940s although a small breeding population has recently been observed in Clark County. A list of wildlife species present in the Complex can be found in Appendix A.

The following synopsis describes various species potentially occurring on Service lands. This information is not intended to represent or describe all species.

Invertebrate Populations

Wetlands associated with Service lands normally carry high invertebrate populations. Nesting waterfowl, waterfowl broods, marsh and water birds, and shorebirds are highly dependent on these protein food sources for healthy, vigorous growth. Invertebrates associated with Complex wetlands include worms, crustaceans, snails, and insects.

Fish Populations

Over 100 species of freshwater fish inhabit South Dakota waters and waterways. Thirty-nine are known, and 68 of these species have the potential, to occur in lakes and wetlands on WMD lands. The fishery associated with Service lands is classified as warm-water with low numbers of game fish and high numbers of minnows, carp, and suckers. Due to the shallow nature of lakes and wetlands, there is a high probability of fish winterkill. The exception are the Refuge lakes which are now part of Waubay Lake due to rising water levels. This lake is currently providing excellent northern pike, walleye, and yellow perch fishing.

Reptiles and Amphibians

Thirty-three species of reptiles occur in South Dakota. Ten are known, and 20 of these species potentially, occur within the Complex. Broad reptile groups include turtles, skinks, and snakes. There are 16 species of amphibians that occur in South Dakota. Eleven could potentially occur on Service lands (Fischer et al. 1999). These species consist of salamanders, toads, and frogs.

Birds

Two-hundred forty-seven bird species are recorded as regularly occurring within the Complex (USFWS 1988). About 109 of these species nest within the Complex. Another 12 species are accidentals or extirpated. A complete listing can be found in Appendix A. Species in the Complex listed in the Office of Migratory Bird Management's "Migratory Nongame Birds of Management Concern in the United States: The 2000 List" (USFWS 2000) are shown with an asterisk in the Appendix.

Waterfowl and Other Water Birds

Waubay Complex lies within the Prairie Pothole Region of North America. This area is of prime importance for producing many of the nation's ducks. In addition, as part of the Central Flyway, other waterfowl species use the area as important stopover sites on migrational routes. The tundra swan is the only species of swan to occur within the Complex. They are most often seen during fall migration. Three species of geese visit the Complex during migration. Canada geese, white-fronted geese, and snow geese pass through in the spring and fall. Canada geese and snow geese are the most abundant species. Canada geese are also common nesters in the area. Duck species that nest in the Complex are: mallard, gadwall, northern pintail, green-winged teal, blue-winged teal, American wigeon, northern shoveler, wood duck, redhead, canvasback, lesser scaup, ring-necked duck, and ruddy duck. Common goldeneye, bufflehead, hooded merganser, common merganser, and red-breasted mergansers migrate through the region.

The diversity of wetlands associated with uplands on Service lands attracts a great variety of shorebirds, wading birds, and passerines. Many shorebirds use the mudflats and shallows along wetland edges or as water levels recede during their migrations in the spring and fall. Wetlands provide breeding habitat for a number of species of marsh and water birds including: eared, horned, red-necked, western, and pied-billed grebes; great blue herons; black-crowned night herons; American bitterns; Virginia rails; soras; American coots; killdeer; upland sandpipers; willets; American avocets; Wilson's phalarope; Franklin's gulls; and Forster's, common, and black terns. Red-winged and yellow-headed blackbirds are quite common in and around wetlands as are marsh and sedge wrens.

Grassland Birds

Since South Dakota is in the Northern Great Plains, grassland birds are the predominant bird life. Grassland bird species are of particular concern since they have shown consistent population declines over the past 30 years (Sauer et al. 1997). Some passerines that depend on grasslands include bobolink; dickcissel; savannah, grasshopper, vesper, and clay-colored sparrows; and western meadowlark. Other species that use grasslands for nesting, feeding, or resting areas include waterfowl, some shorebirds and wading birds, as well as short-eared owl, northern harrier, and Swainson's hawk. Sharp-tailed grouse are common upland species that nest within the Complex. The greater prairie chicken historically nested in the region, and a small breeding population was recently found in Clark County.

The brown-headed cowbird is a grassland species whose range has exploded across most of North America in response to the conversion of forests to farms and pastures. Once associated with the moving herds of bison, it is now less migratory and has successfully parasitized 144 of 220 species in whose nests its eggs have been found (Ehrlich et al. 1988). Cowbirds can be particularly destructive to the reproductive success of species that have not evolved or learned to recognize the foreign eggs. Cowbird eggs generally hatch one day earlier than host eggs and the larger, more aggressive cowbird young will out compete the host species hatchlings for food. Species that may be susceptible to cowbird parasitism include yellow warblers, red-eyed and warbling vireos, and song sparrows.

Other Migratory Birds

Raptors including eagles, hawks, falcons, and owls are found on the Complex. The most common are the red-tailed hawk, northern harrier, and Swainson's hawk. Smaller hawks, such as Cooper's and sharp-shinned hawks, and American kestrels have been documented as nesting in the Complex. The most common owl is the great horned owl. Other species that might be seen during migrations include osprey, northern goshawk, broad-winged hawk, and prairie falcon.

Refuge woodlands and area coulees provide habitat for many migrating warblers including palm, Tennessee, orange-crowned, yellow-rumped, mourning, blackpoll, and black-and-white warblers. They also provide habitat for yellow warblers, red-eyed and warbling vireos, rose-breasted grosbeaks, hairy and downy woodpeckers, black-capped chickadees, and numerous other woodland species.

No long-term studies of avian communities have been conducted in wooded draws. Casual observations have found five species of warblers during spring migration as well as reports of turkey vultures and pileated woodpeckers in wooded coulees in Roberts County. One study of woodland types in the Little Missouri National Grasslands found that certain neotropical migrants (red-eyed vireo, black-and-white warbler, yellow-breasted chat, American redstart, lazuli bunting, rufous-sided towhee, lark sparrow, and American goldfinch) were significantly more abundant in ash woodlands than in juniper, pine or even cottonwood habitats (Hopkins et al. 1986).

Mammals

An estimated 43 mammal species are found within the six county Waubay Complex. They range in size from tiny shrews weighing an ounce or less to large ungulates, such as the common white-tailed deer or the rarely seen wandering moose, weighing hundreds of pounds. Abundance varies with species. Prairie insectivores and native mice common to prairie ecosystems are very abundant, and species like the opossum and some species of bats are very uncommon on Service lands. No State or Federal endangered or threatened mammals are known to occur in Waubay Complex.

State and Federal Endangered and Threatened Species

Bald eagles, a federally listed threatened species, are an uncommon migrant throughout the State, but can winter in large numbers along the Missouri River (South Dakota Ornithologists' Union 1991). They were historically a rare breeder in the extreme southeast part of the State. Bald eagles were previously only seen during migration in Waubay WMD, but within the last 3 years, pairs have been found nesting in Roberts and Marshall Counties.

Piping plovers, a federally threatened species in South Dakota, are a locally common resident albeit primarily in the Missouri River valley. They are generally an uncommon migrant elsewhere in the State and have nested in Day and Codington counties only rarely (South Dakota Ornithologists' Union 1991). The last known nesting attempt in Day County occurred in 1985 between North and South Waubay lakes (SDGFP 1994). Loss of breeding and wintering habitat are its biggest threats. It needs open sand and gravel beaches with sparse vegetation for nesting and is a common breeding associate with the interior least tern.

The whooping crane, a federally listed endangered species, only rarely passes through the Complex during its migration. Most sightings occur farther west in the State. The most recent sighting in the WMD was in Clark County in fall of 2000. Before that, whooping cranes hadn't been seen in the District since 1985. The Eskimo curlew, endangered, is nearly extinct. They pass through the Great Plains on their migrations and can potentially occur in wet meadows within the Complex. The interior least tern, endangered, nests along the Missouri River in central South Dakota. It is an uncommon migrant in this area.

The osprey is a state threatened species whose numbers were drastically reduced as a result of DDT use in the country. It is an uncommon migrant throughout the state and previously nested in the southeastern part of the state (South Dakota Ornithologists' Union 1991), with a confirmed nest record in the Black Hills in 1991 (Peterson 1995). More recently in Waubay WMD, it has been reported during the spring, late summer, and fall in scattered locations, mostly in Day County.

The American burying beetle, an endangered species, was once common over most of eastern North America. It has since disappeared from over 90 percent of its historic range (Lomolino and Creighton 1996). Hypotheses explaining its widespread decline range from deforestation (Anderson 1982) to loss of available carrion in the required size (especially with the extirpation of passenger pigeons and greater prairie chicken) and increased competition for these resources from other scavengers such as raccoons, fox, and skunks (Amaral et al. 1997). Recent trapping efforts have found American burying beetles in extreme south central South Dakota, primarily in Tripp and Gregory counties (Backlund and Marrone 1995). A trapline set up on the Refuge in 1996 produced no American Burying beetles. Additional surveys should be done to completely rule out the presence of this endangered species. Current management tools used, especially prescribed burns and pesticides, could negatively affect invertebrate populations. Not knowing for sure if American burying beetles are present or how they may be affected by current practices leaves this species at risk.

The Topeka shiner is the only federally listed endangered fish species that may occur on the Complex. Although it was believed to be missing from much of its historic locations in South Dakota, recent surveys found healthy populations in many of the tributaries of the James, Vermillion and Big Sioux Rivers. As an indicator of stream health, finding the Topeka shiner suggests these systems are still relatively intact. Locating the Topeka shiner is the first step to protecting vital waterways and watersheds which sustain native fisheries as well as the human populations which also depend on clean water.

No federally listed reptiles or amphibians have been observed. The only State threatened species in this region is the northern redbelly snake. The usual habitat for this snake is moist woodlands. Waubay NWR is known to host this snake.

The Dakota skipper butterfly is listed as imperiled in South Dakota because of its rarity and vulnerability to extinction. It was also considered for Federal listing under the Endangered Species Act. Other rare prairie-dependent butterfly species found in the Complex include the powesheik skipper and the regal fritillary. Generally, large, undisturbed native prairie tracts are required habitat for these species. Management of sites where these butterflies are found will need to be adjusted to protect these species. Primarily, sites should be divided into smaller management units, to prevent management activities, such as burning or haying, from affecting the whole unit at once.

State threatened fish species that may occur on Service lands include the northern redbelly dace and trout-perch. State endangered species include the central mudminnow and the banded killifish.

Cultural Resources

A 1981 archaeological survey by Keller and Zimmerman found 27 archaeological resource sites on the Refuge. Their cultural inventory report concluded that four sites were significant resources. Artifacts found included lithics, ceramics, animal remains, and stone tools.

Additional sites exist in Day and Marshall Counties. The Waubay Complex lies within the Upper James, Prairie Coteau, Upper Big Sioux, and Northeast Lowland Archaeological Regions of the State. Documented occupation of the area spans a 10,000-year period. Significant cultural resources are probably present on some of the thousands of acres of native prairie. The Regional Archaeologist is consulted during the planning phase of any proposed project. The need for a cultural resource inventory is determined in consultation with the South Dakota Historic Preservation Office.

Public Use

The majority of outdoor recreational uses in northeast South Dakota are centered around fishing and hunting. Numerous glacial lakes provide many opportunities for fishing in the area. Due to the increase in water levels, Waubay Lake has become a premier fishery, featured in several sportsmen's magazines. In the past, the Complex was also well-known for its ring-necked pheasant and white-tailed deer hunting. Pheasant populations are recovering slowly from a low in 1997. Deer are still abundant, but many of the trophy bucks have been harvested due to a lack of emergent vegetation, which was used as escape cover. The area also offers some of South Dakota's finest waterfowl hunting and other small game hunting which attracts hunters from all parts of the United States. Many public lands provide the quality and quantity of hunting sites needed for residents and visitors to use.

Other outdoor activities such as photography, camping, hiking, and bird-watching are also popular in this region. The South Dakota Game, Fish and Parks Department has many State Parks and Recreation Areas that are used primarily in spring, summer, and fall seasons for these activities.

Facilities for visitors to Service lands are somewhat limited. Information kiosks with leaflet dispensers are located at the Headquarters building and tower. Refuge entrances and boundaries are marked with signs; limited directional and regulation signs are on the Refuge. A Visitor Center is located in the Headquarters building which provides information and exhibits for Refuge visitors. However, the building is currently only open during regular office hours (Monday-Friday 8:00 am to 4:30 pm), with no weekend hours. Two walking trails are available during daylight hours. One is ½ mile long and is located near the Headquarters building. A portion of this trail is accessible to persons with disabilities. The other trail travels ¼ mile up a small hill for a view of Spring Lake and native prairie. Both trails include interpretive signs. A 110-foot observation tower is also open for public use providing panoramic views of the Refuge and surrounding area.

All WPAs have boundary signs. No kiosks or designated hiking trails are located on WPAs. There are eight redwood recognition signs in the WMD that acknowledge from whom the Service purchased the property. These are usually located along well-traveled highways. Grassed parking lots are located at many of the larger WPAs to provide off-road parking.

Without a person on staff dedicated to public use, environmental education opportunities on the Complex are limited. Currently, these duties tend to fall on the wildlife biologist or any of the managers on staff. Talks and tours are offered at the Refuge when requested, if no conflicts occur with other duties. Programs offered to area schools or communities are also offered on an availability basis. Oftentimes, only a few programs are presented each year. Through an agreement with Ne-So-Dak's Glacial Lakes Outdoor School, educators from Ne-So-Dak use the Refuge as a base for their environmental education efforts. Approximately 250 to 350 school-age children visit the Refuge each year thanks to this partnership.

Economic Environment

The Refuge is in Day County, approximately 25 miles northeast of the city of Webster, the county seat and biggest town in the county, with a population of 2,200. The rural population is very sparse due to its agricultural nature. Recent low farm prices, coupled with water inundating many acres of cropland, have put a strain on the local economy.

Approximately 2.6 percent of the land in the six county WMD is owned by State or Federal agencies. To help achieve goals and objectives, upland habitat management is often accomplished by authorizing local farmers to hay or graze on Service lands. Weed control also helps economically by protecting neighboring land from infestation by noxious weeds. Surrounding landowners and economies may also be assisted through development of new weed control methods such as using flea beetles or other management tools and techniques.

The economy of the area is based primarily on ranching and tourism. Waubay Complex contributes to the local economy primarily by attracting tourists, bird-watchers, and hunters. The State collects hunting license fees for deer hunting on the Refuge. In 1999 the receipts for Refuge deer licenses totaled $4,270. Many out-of-state and resident hunters are drawn to the WMD for public waterfowl hunting. Most of them will spend money in this area for licenses, motels, food, fuel, and other hunting necessities. The permitting of some grazing and haying on Service lands benefits the local economy. In 1999 nearly 4,000 acres in the WMD were grazed, 67 were hayed, and 18 were farmed. Payments made to counties in-lieu of taxes for Service lands also provide economic benefit. In 1998 these payments totaled $50,513.

Interstate 29 cuts through the center of the WMD, north and south. U.S. Highways 12 and 212 go through east to west. The nearest airport with scheduled passenger service is in Watertown, the Codington County seat. Codington is the fifth most populated county in the State.

Most of the land adjacent to the Refuge is in private ownership. The Sisseton-Wahpeton Tribal boundary borders the Refuge to the east.

Special Designations

The woodland north of Hillebrand's Lake is designated by the Society of American Foresters as a Research Natural Area because of its unique bur oak/little bluestem cover type. No special management occurs due to the designation.

To be considered for Wilderness designation a site must be greater than 5,000 acres. No lands in the Complex qualify for this designation. No rivers qualify for Wild and Scenic River status.

IV. Management Direction

The Complex planning team defined goals for four main categories: habitat, wildlife, cultural resources, and wildlife-dependent recreation. Objectives and strategies are further refinements of each goal. The most extensive section concerns habitat, with the assumption that good habitat management should bring a corresponding response from wildlife populations. Managing habitat is often more controllable than wildlife population management, which may be subject to regional or continental influences beyond the control of localized management efforts. For example, management for tall, dense, diverse grasslands may not bring a corresponding increase in waterfowl during a drought cycle, when these birds also are dependent on abundant wetland resources.

Goals and objectives are presented separately for Waubay National Wildlife Refuge and Waubay Wetland Management District for ease of understanding and reference. (NWR goals are designated with an "R" while WMD goals are designated with a "D.") However, the NWR and WMD are interrelated in many ways. Waubay NWR is located nearly in the center of Waubay WMD, and its habitats and wildlife are similar. The major building facilities (headquarters, shop, storage buildings) are physically located on Waubay NWR, but most staff activities, equipment, and facilities are associated with WMD programs. At present, all staff work on both NWR and WMD activities.

The biggest concerns for the Complex include protecting remaining native prairie, increasing biodiversity by restoring tame grasslands to native species, protecting and providing habitat for waterfowl and other migratory birds, protecting and restoring wetlands, and providing increased opportunities for public use, environmental education, and interpretation. There is also a concern for native woodlands in the Complex - a little studied or understood resource in this area.

> "Those who dwell, as scientists or laymen, among the beauties and mysteries of the earth are never alone or weary of life. Those who contemplate the beauty of the earth find reserves of strength that will endure as long as life lasts."
> Rachel Carson

Waubay National Wildlife Refuge
Habitat

■ *R1 - Habitat Goal: To preserve, restore and enhance the ecological diversity of grasslands, wetlands, and native woodlands of the Prairie Pothole Region of the Great Plains on Waubay National Wildlife Refuge.*

Grasslands

According to a 1948 Refuge land use plan, much of the Refuge had been farmed or heavily grazed prior to acquisition. The dominant Refuge upland cover types are native prairie (1,109 acres) and native trees (494 acres). However, the high water period of the late 1990s inundated 941 acres of native prairie (Thanapura 1998), much of it diverse tallgrass communities adjacent to Refuge lakes. Currently, there are 1,371 acres of grassland on the Refuge, including 262 acres of tame grasses, dense nesting cover, or old alfalfa fields. Old alfalfa fields (69 acres), heavily invaded by brome and quack grass, are included in the grassland totals.

Objectives

R1.1 Annually convert up to 50 acres of tame grasses, dense nesting cover, or old alfalfa fields to native plant communities, including forbs, until reaching a total of 262 acres.

> Rationale for Objective: The most abundant introduced grasses, especially Kentucky bluegrass and smooth brome, tend to be more uniform in height and density than native species (Wilson and Belcher 1989). This uniformity may produce changes in nongame bird species composition (Wilson and Belcher 1989). Conservation of grassland-dependent bird species and other wildlife depend on a variety of successional and diverse habitat conditions within a large block of grass (Skinner et al. 1984, Volkert 1992, Madden 1996). Several bird species, such as dickcissel and savannah sparrow, are most abundant in fields with a strong forb component (Sample and Mossman 1997). Forbs are also needed to provide nectar and larval host plants for butterflies. Three Refuge species considered at risk in the Dakotas (Moffat and McPhillips 1993) include the regal fritillary, Dakota and powesheik skippers. Restored native prairie tracts can provide more variety in structure, height, and species than is found in most monotypic tame stands, better emulating native prairie.

> Strategies:
> ■ Research appropriate native seed mixes and their availability, within one year.
> ■ Prioritize areas of tame grasses, dense nesting cover, and old alfalfa fields for conversion.
> ■ Develop management plans to monitor restored native grasslands for weeds, grassland condition, and wildlife response.

R1.2 Eliminate 95 percent of Russian olive and juniper stands and reduce by 50 percent other nonnative plants, such as leafy spurge and Canada thistle, over the next 15 years.

> Rationale for Objective: For grassland obligate wildlife species, woody vegetation should cover less than 5 percent of available habitat (Sample and Mossman 1997). Nonnative junipers, Russian olives, and other woody vegetation, especially those over 1 meter (39 inches) in height in grasslands, can provide habitat for nest parasites, predators, and corridors for predator movement (Berkey et al. 1993). Removing woody vegetation can improve nesting habitat and success for waterfowl and other grassland species. Nonnative plants, such as Canada thistle and leafy spurge, have no natural controls in the United States and can aggressively invade grasslands, reducing biodiversity and structure necessary for healthy grasslands and wildlife species.

Strategies:
- Inventory and map existing distribution of nonnative plants, within 5 years.
- Use a combination of biological, chemical, and mechanical means; with an emphasis on biological control for leafy spurge.

R1.3 Within 5 years, develop and implement a Habitat Management Plan for the Refuge.

> Rationale for Objective: Developing unit-specific habitat management plans will increase staff effectiveness and habitat conditions by setting priorities and ensuring actions are directed towards the most critical areas on the Refuge first. Documenting and monitoring changes improves the ability of staff to relate specific management tools to on-the-ground results.

Strategies:
- Develop individual unit plans for management, biological inventories, and monitoring activities to be carried out on each grassland unit on the Refuge. Unit plans would determine current grassland condition and decide management course of action.
- Establish monitoring criteria to evaluate grassland management techniques, within 5 years.
- Manage tame grassland sites not scheduled for conversion to natives for maximum potential height and density based on grass species involved and site conditions. Strive for two decimeters (8 inches) of total visual obstruction in mid-April, as suggested for optimal nesting habitat for waterfowl (Duebbert et al. 1981).
- Develop prescribed burn plans for all grassland units which would benefit from periodic burning.

Wetlands

During "normal" water conditions, there are approximately 1,800 acres of wetlands on the Refuge. About 12 acres were considered temporary, 90 acres seasonal, 192 acres as semipermanent, and 1,500 acres as permanent lakes. High water conditions which began in the mid-1990s have increased wet acreage (mostly lake acreage) by another 400 to 500 acres. Many semipermanent wetlands have been swallowed up and are currently included as part of Waubay Lake, which also now includes Spring and Hillebrand's Lakes. These changes have resulted in an increase in water depths and a corresponding decrease in submergent and emergent vegetation. This means there is less feeding and nesting habitat for diving ducks and over-water nesters such as red-necked grebes, but more habitat for pelicans, double-crested cormorants, and wood ducks. It is anticipated that current high water levels will continue for at least 15 years, the life of this plan (Niehus et al. 1999, 1999a).

There are three water control structures located on the Refuge. One is completely inundated by the extreme water levels and will not be replaced or repaired when water levels recede. Another, which affects approximately three acres, is located along the entrance road and is in need of repair. It will be replaced with an ordinary culvert to reduce maintenance problems and protect the road. The third is located on Barse Slough, a 15 acre wetland on the east side of the Refuge. Some minor repairs are needed to make this structure fully functional.

Objective

R1.4 Enhance wetland conditions on 15 managed acres by allowing them to flood each spring and slowly drawing down water levels to expose mudflats and provide shallow water areas, 15 cm (6 inches), for waterfowl and shorebird feeding during spring migrations.

> Rationale for Objective: Water control structures can increase the productivity of a wetland by allowing managers to change water levels to affect the types and amount of vegetation that grows in the wetland. In fact, in many wetlands, active management may be necessary to maintain desirable species and communities (Baldassarre and Bolen 1994). Managed wetlands may also be able to provide habitat that might be in short supply due to overall climatic conditions. However, there is no water source for reflooding this wetland, it is dependent on spring snowmelt and rains. Providing habitat for fall migration by drawing down in the summer and reflooding in fall would be difficult if not impossible some years. Since this structure only affects 15 acres, providing emergent cover for nesting or brooding waterfowl or other waterbirds would not affect a large number of birds. At this time, mudflats and shallow water areas are in short supply and providing this habitat during spring migration could help numerous waterbirds, especially prenesting females. Drawing down water levels will also help to concentrate macroinvertebrates and other food sources for migratory birds.

> Strategies:
> - Monitor site frequently to make adjustments to water level depths for optimum plant and macroinvertebrate production as determined by standard methods.
> - Maintain records of responses by plants and animals to determine if changes need to be made in timing or frequency of drawdowns.

Native Woodlands

There are approximately 500 acres of native bur oak woodlands on the Refuge. The overstory consists mostly of bur oak, green ash, basswood, elm, and hackberry. The understory includes choke cherry, buffalo berry, Juneberry (serviceberry), and buckbrush. Ground cover is dominated by sedges and stinging nettle. Before the establishment of the Refuge, food plots of 10 to 30 acres in size were cut out of three woodland areas (West Woods, Centerwoods, and Clubhouse Woods). After the Refuge was established, these three fields continued to be used for wildlife food plots. Rye was planted in the fall for green browse, then plowed under in spring and planted to millet, which was left standing for wildlife (D. Okroi, pers. comm.). When waters began rising these areas were planted to alfalfa as staff realized getting equipment to these soon to be isolated sites would be impossible.

Objectives
R1.5 Restore native trees on 3 food plots of 10 to 30 acres in size (total of 50 acres) within the Refuge's native woodlands (Map 6), within 15 years, to decrease fragmentation to reduce brown-headed cowbird populations and increase woodland bird species and their nesting success.

> Rationale for Objective: From 1994 to 1996 a constant effort mist netting site was set up in Centerwoods. Data collected also contributed to the Monitoring Avian Productivity and Survivorship (MAPS) program. Point counts were conducted in conjunction with the mist netting. Results averaging the 3 years of point counts showed brown-headed cowbirds were the second most abundant species observed, after red-winged blackbirds. They also made up nearly 6 percent of total captures in mist nets. Even though yellow warblers comprised 10 percent of total captures, only one hatch year bird was banded during this study period. Yellow warblers are one of the three most frequent cowbird hosts (Ehrlich et al. 1988) and the high abundance of cowbirds may be affecting yellow warbler nest success in this area. Nests that occur along forest edges and in small forest patches experience greater rates of nest predation (Wilcove 1985, Yahner and Scott 1988) and brood parasitism by brown-headed cowbirds (Brittingham and Temple 1983, Gates and Gysel 1978). Replanting the old farm fields will reduce edges and increase effective woodland size, thereby reducing negative edge effects and possibly brood parasitism.

Strategies:
- Replant old farm fields located on Headquarters, Centerwoods, and West Woods islands to native trees.
- Monitor, with point counts, changes in bird populations as reforestation progresses.
- Research appropriate methods, such as field preparation and tree species to use within 5 years.

R1.6 Develop and implement a Habitat Management Plan (HMP) for oak savannah and eastern deciduous forest types, within 5 years, to protect and sustain these important habitats for migratory birds and other wildlife.

Rationale for Objective: Few management plans have been developed specifically for Refuge woodlands, although they encompass nearly one third of upland habitats. Forest management is generally outside the scope of current staff and most of their time is dedicated to wetland and grassland habitats. Although a few prescribed burns have been executed in and around woodland areas, little is known about the effects these burns have had or how best to continue management of these areas. Consulting with people more knowledgeable in this field and developing long-term management plans can provide benefits to many species that inhabit these sites. Some woodland-dependent bird species that currently occur on the Refuge that could benefit from improved management include black-billed cuckoo, Cooper's hawk, least and great-crested flycatchers, red-eyed and warbling vireos, yellow warbler, northern oriole, and rose-breasted grosbeak.

Strategies:
- Use GIS or other methods to map forest types.
- Consult forestry experts to help formulate forestry management plans.
- Maintain 60 acres of rotating food plots (outside forest areas), annually, to reduce browse pressure on woodlands from wintering deer.
- Develop research study to determine impact of white-tailed deer to forests and possible strategies to minimize these impacts.

Wildlife

- *R2 - Wildlife Goal: To promote a natural diversity and abundance of native flora and fauna of the Prairie Pothole Region of the Great Plains on Waubay National Wildlife Refuge.*

Because wildlife populations are dynamic and can be affected by factors such as weather, disease, pollution or other factors outside of human control, the following objectives focus primarily on increasing our knowledge of wildlife needs and monitoring wildlife populations and land use patterns in order to better direct habitat management.

Objectives
R2.1 Within the 15 year life of this plan, conserve habitat capable of achieving a waterfowl recruitment rate of 0.49 under average environmental conditions.

> Rationale for Objective: This is a step-down objective from the U.S. Prairie Pothole Joint Venture (PPJV) Implementation Plan. The PPJV itself is a step-down plan from the North American Waterfowl Management Plan. Both plans focus on protecting, restoring, and enhancing wetlands and grasslands in order to achieve waterfowl population objectives. Accordingly, this CCP also focuses on providing quality habitat for waterfowl.

Strategies:
- Preserve, restore, and enhance wetland and grassland habitat as outlined in objectives R1.1, R1.3, and R1.4.

R2.2 Develop an Inventory and Monitoring Plan, within 3 years, to locate and track specific locations used by the following endangered or threatened species: bald eagle, piping plover, American burying beetle, and western prairie fringed orchid.

Rationale for Objective: The species listed above may potentially use the Refuge for some part of their life-cycles. Bald eagles were previously only seen during migration on the Refuge and in the District, but within the last 3 years, nesting pairs have been found in Roberts and Marshall Counties. Sightings of bald eagles are also becoming more common during summer months (Refuge files).

Piping plovers rarely nested in Day and Codington counties (South Dakota Ornithologists' Union 1991), with the last known nesting attempt in 1985 between North and South Waubay Lakes (SDGFP 1994). Major habitat changes have occurred since then, reducing available sand or gravel beaches preferred for nesting. However, even small reductions in water levels now can open up new nesting sites for these birds. Monitoring for these changes can help to protect future nesting pairs.

Recent trapping efforts have found American burying beetles in extreme south central South Dakota, primarily in Tripp and Gregory counties (Backlund and Marrone 1995). A trapline set-up on the Refuge in 1996 produced no American burying beetles. However, their presence cannot be ruled out without further surveys. Knowing of their presence and locations will help Refuge managers avoid adversely affecting them through actions such as prescribed burning and pesticide application.

The Western prairie fringed orchid is the only known federally threatened plant species that may be present on the Refuge. Historical locations have included sites in the Big Sioux River valley in the southeastern part of South Dakota. It occurs in moist, tallgrass prairies and sedge meadows, both of which can be found on the Complex. It appears to have been extirpated from South Dakota, but remote populations may have been overlooked as it does occur in adjacent counties of Minnesota, North Dakota, Iowa, and Nebraska.

Strategies:
- Protect Refuge sites used by endangered and threatened species.
- Monitor public use of documented sites for adverse impacts and restrict access if and when necessary to minimize disturbance and habitat degradation.
- Use appropriate management techniques and timing to help ensure continued survival of these species.

R2.3 Develop an Inventory and Monitoring Plan, within 3 years, to locate and track specific locations used by the following State species at risk: regal fritillary, Dakota skipper, and powesheik skipper butterflies; osprey; northern redbelly snake; banded killifish; and central mudminnow.

Rationale for Objective: South Dakota's endangered species law was passed in 1977 to ensure the protection of threatened and endangered species within the state. The Game, Fish, and Parks Commission reviews the list of species every 2 years with species added or deleted depending on their vulnerability, with the Game, Fish and Parks Department in charge of the protection of listed species. The South Dakota Natural Heritage Program also documents and monitors over 400 plant and animal species considered at risk in South Dakota. Ongoing monitoring is achieved through the cooperation of various agencies and individuals and helps to keep species from declining to the point where they must be listed. We can further this goal by monitoring these species as well as limiting or adjusting habitat management efforts to reduce potential negative impacts.

Certain species may also serve as indicators of the health of an ecosystem, such as butterflies. Butterflies are part of the prairie ecosystem. If these species are in trouble, other endemic (and harder to track) species may also be in decline. Tracking these butterflies and adjusting management to benefit them should benefit other prairie endemics, improve the health of the prairie ecosystem, and help to prevent the listing of these and other species that have declined due to the poor health of prairie habitats.

Strategies:
- Initiate surveys during appropriate flight times to monitor presence, abundance, and locations of at risk butterfly species.
- Protect Refuge sites where the above mentioned species are located.
- Monitor public use of documented sites for adverse impacts and restrict access if and when necessary to minimize disturbance and habitat degradation.
- Use appropriate management techniques and timing to ensure continued survival of these species at risk.

R2.4 Rewrite and update the Wildlife Inventory Plan to include methodology for a variety of surveys, increasing the number and quality of surveys of residential and migratory wildlife species, within 10 years.

Rationale for Objective: Incredible habitat changes have occurred since 1968 and 1972 when the Wildlife Inventory Plan for Waubay NWR was written and last amended. The CCP provides an opportunity to update the Plan. Better quality surveys will increase the staff's knowledge of Refuge use patterns by resident and migratory species. Past surveys have concentrated on waterfowl and deer with little effort devoted to other birds or wildlife besides casual observations. Newly developed refuge management plans and looking at regional plans developed by The Nature Conservancy, Partners in Flight, Prairie Pothole Joint Venture, and others, will help to direct which species would best benefit from monitoring. Continued participation in cooperative surveys helps to contribute to long-term national databases and a larger scale understanding of wildlife populations. These surveys can help staff understand the Refuge's role regionally, and to develop local goals and objectives. White-tailed deer populations are regulated by the South Dakota Game, Fish and Parks. Cooperation with them is essential for providing recreation and keeping deer herds in check to reduce depredation complaints and habitat destruction.

Strategies:
- Continue participation in cooperative surveys such as the Christmas Bird Count.
- Cooperate with SDGFP on deer surveys and population management.
- Review regional and national plans to help determine how to broaden surveys, for which species.
- Research and determine appropriate survey methodologies for habitats and species targeted.

Cultural Resources

- *R3 - Cultural Resources Goal: Protect and interpret significant historic and prehistoric cultural resources associated with Waubay National Wildlife Refuge.*

In 1981 a complete survey for cultural resources was conducted on the Refuge (Keller and Zimmerman 1981) as well as other partial surveys (Zimmerman et al. 1978, Winham 1983, Bradley and Ranney 1985). A total of 27 sites were found: 14 prehistoric and 13 historic. Most of the prehistoric sites consist of mounds or habitation sites from several major cultural groups, including the Plains Woodland and Plains Village cultures (Keller and Zimmerman 1981). The historic sites are mostly foundations of destroyed structures from early homesteads or farms inhabited prior to the establishment of the Refuge.

Jackson and Toom (1999) believed that Keller and Zimmerman (1981) misinterpreted the guidelines of the National Register of Historic Places (NRHP) since they believed the four major Refuge prehistoric sites were not eligible for nomination to NRHP. Jackson and Toom pointed out that NRHP eligibility was not limited to just national significance, but also can be evaluated on the basis of local or state importance (National Park Service 1998).

Historic sites, mostly old foundations, dating from around 1900, were submitted by the Service for NRHP eligibility, but were found not to be significant resources. However, the major prehistoric sites were not submitted to NRHP.

Objectives

R3.1 Within the 15 year life of this plan, locate, map, and determine NRHP eligibility of all significant historic and prehistoric cultural and archaeological resources on the Refuge.

> Rationale for Objective: All sites should be relocated and reevaluated as to their current condition and protection needs. Unfortunately, some of the sites have probably been covered or partially covered by high water levels. Sites that are under water should be monitored closely for the appearance of artifacts and other important materials. Jackson and Toom (1999) believe that most of the archaeological sites should be reevaluated to determine their NRHP eligibility. Most of the historic sites are likely ineligible. The information revealed from these sites can help guide current and future management by providing a historical background of habitats, wildlife, and cultural uses which shaped this land and the changes that have occurred since then.

Strategies:

- Nominate for listing on the NRHP the four major prehistoric archaeological sites.
- Reevaluate and record the remaining documented sites to determine official NRHP status.
- Produce a cultural resource overlay for Geographic Information System (GIS) database.
- Consult with the Regional Historic Preservation Officer prior to all proposed actions.
- Monitor sites that are now under water and exposed shorelines as water levels recede for the appearance of artifacts and other important materials.
- Avoid areas of known cultural sites and potential sensitive areas when practical and mitigate any adverse effects to sites.
- Utilize standard law enforcement practices and strategies to protect cultural resources already identified and those that may be discovered where development of water control structures, wetland restorations, and other ground breaking activities will occur.

R3.2 Interpret the cultural resources of the Refuge for visitors of all ages and abilities through at least 3 exhibits within 7 years.

Rationale for Objective: Prehistoric and historic cultural sites can provide a fascinating wealth of information about the history of this area and the people and cultures that inhabited it. They help us learn how these cultures related to wildlife and the environment. Interpreting these sites will allow the public to learn more about this history and these relationships. This can often be an important step to understanding and developing solutions to current issues. Partnering with the Sisseton-Wahpeton Sioux Tribe will give a vital perspective often missing in cultural interpretation.

Strategies:
- Upgrade Refuge kiosk exhibit as advised in the 2001 Visitor Services Requirement report prepared by the regional Education and Visitor Services group.
- Upgrade Refuge visitor center exhibit as advised in the 2001 Visitor Services Requirement report.
- Investigate establishment of a cooperative interpretive site with Sisseton-Wahpeton Sioux Tribe.
- Ensure all new visitor materials and facilities reach the broadest audience possible by following the Universal Design concept.
- Incorporate interpretation of Wetland Management District cultural resources into the Refuge program, presenting a more comprehensive interpretive program.

Public Use and Education

■ *R4 - Wildlife-dependent Recreation Goal: To foster an understanding and appreciation of the ecology and management of the fauna and flora and of the role of humans in the Prairie Pothole Region of the Great Plains by providing Refuge visitors of all abilities with compatible wildlife-dependent recreational experiences.*

In 1997, the National Wildlife Refuge System Improvement Act was signed into law. In addition to establishing a mission for the NWRS, it also determined that wildlife-dependent recreation, when compatible with a Refuge's purpose, are legitimate uses and should be facilitated where appropriate. Priority wildlife-dependent uses include hunting, fishing, wildlife observation, wildlife photography, environmental education and interpretation.

Hunting

Three types of deer hunting are allowed on the Refuge: archery, rifle, and black-powder rifle (or muzzleloaders). Bows and black-powder rifles are considered primitive weapons. Modern rifles are more effective for controlling herd numbers than either of the primitive weapons. Currently, no separate archery season occurs on the Refuge. Anyone with an east river or Statewide tag may archery hunt on the Refuge. In Day County, and others, there is also an antlerless deer tag offered for archery hunters. This season runs from late September through mid-January. These tags can also be used on the Refuge.

For muzzleloader hunters, the Refuge offers two 5-day seasons for any deer before the regular rifle seasons (Refuge or State). The State only offers a late December to January hunt for antlerless only deer. Since most tags are sold each season, Refuge hunts appear to be attractive to hunters.

Waterfowl hunting is not allowed on the Refuge for several reasons. Abundant waterfowl hunting opportunities exist in the six county area around the Refuge, including 40,000 acres of Waterfowl Production Areas managed by the Service, 46,700 acres of state-managed public hunting areas, and 88,700 acres of public walk-in areas, for a total of 175,400 acres. South Dakota Game, Fish and Parks realizes the need to maintain closed areas to allow migrating birds to rest during the hunting season and currently manages six waterfowl refuges closed to hunting, with Waubay NWR providing another closed area for waterfowl. The Service has developed retrieval zones on prime hunting areas along Refuge boundaries to facilitate hunting on neighboring lands.

Pheasant hunting is also not allowed on the Refuge. Waubay NWR and the immediate surrounding area is marginal pheasant habitat. In 2002, less than a dozen pheasants were found on the Refuge, numbers too low to warrant a hunt. Additionally, as with waterfowl hunting, 175,400 acres in the six county area are already open to pheasant hunting.

Objective

R4.1 Regulate hunter numbers to no more than one hunter per 100 acres of upland deer habitat to provide safe, quality, deer hunting experiences.

Rationale for Objective: Before 1939, white-tailed deer did not occur on the Refuge (Revised Master Economic Use Plan 1949, Refuge Files). Since then, deer herds have grown and have taken a toll on Refuge woodlands and surrounding lands, especially during harsh winters. The objectives for white-tailed deer hunting on the Refuge are to keep deer herds in check to protect Refuge and surrounding habitat, and to provide quality recreational opportunities. The Refuge is also used for protection and feeding by wintering deer herds. These needs must be considered when developing season lengths as well as any conflicts with other public uses, such as ice fishing. License numbers are based on past season hunting success, winter survival, herd size, and the desire to maintain a quality, uncrowded hunting experience.

Strategies:

- Work with South Dakota Game, Fish and Parks to annually evaluate permit numbers, season lengths, and types.
- Work with South Dakota Game, Fish and Parks to conduct law enforcement patrols to ensure regulation compliance and to provide a safe experience for all visitors.
- Maintain designated hunting parking areas.
- Identify areas open to hunting and inform the public about Refuge hunting regulations and access through signs, news releases, and pamphlets.
- Consider limiting the season length of the archery antlerless deer season, currently late September to mid-January, in order to make sure wintering deer herds are not overly disturbed later in the season.
- Investigate feasibility of offering hunts for people with disabilities and youth.
- Continue to promote primitive weapon (archery, black-powder rifle) Refuge deer hunts.

Fishing

Before 1997, no sustainable fishery existed on Refuge lakes. Shallowness and a tendency to winterkill prevented any sport fish populations from developing. Since Spring and Hillebrand Lakes have merged with Waubay Lake, populations of perch, walleye, northern pike, and others have grown dramatically and inhabit all corners of this 20,000-acre lake system. Some 2,500 to 3,000 acres of the Waubay Lake system currently occur within Refuge boundaries.

Fishing is one of the priority public uses as outlined in the Refuge Improvement Act of 1997. However, all uses must be considered compatible with the mission of the System and the Refuge's purpose, namely "a refuge and breeding ground for migratory birds and wildlife." The productivity, abundance, and distribution of waterbirds can be impacted by fishing activities (Bell and Austin 1985, Edwards and Bell 1985, Cooke 1987, Bouffard 1982). Waterfowl tend to be wary of any disturbance, especially that associated with loud noise and rapid movement (Korschgen and Dahlgren 1992). Cooke (1987) also found that anglers on shore or in a boat tend to fish the same areas that birds favor, namely shallow, sheltered bays and creeks. Johnson (1964) also found that breeding, feeding, or resting waterfowl will be disturbed often by anglers in boats or on shore. Human disturbances to breeding waterfowl can affect numbers of breeding pairs, cause increased desertion of nests, reduce hatching success and decrease duckling survival (Korschgen and Dahlgren 1992, Beard 1953, Barngrover 1974, Jahn and Hunt 1964, Keith 1961). Migrating birds may also be negatively affected by increasing energy expenditures and depleting fat reserves and prolonged disturbances can ultimately affect migration patterns (Evenson 1974, Heitmeyer 1985, Korschgen et al., 1985). Recreational activities can also have detrimental effects on plants (both on and offshore) and water quality (Liddle and Scorgie 1980).

Shoreline fishing offers several problems in addition to waterfowl disturbance. There is only one area accessible to the public for shoreline fishing, the headquarters road. Large numbers of vehicles would park along this road due to a lack of parking areas. To build more parking areas would necessitate destroying native prairie. Secondly, this road would be very susceptible to damage from vehicles being parked on the shoulders during wet conditions. This road is vitally important since it is the only link to the outside for all the facilities and equipment housed at the headquarters area. Erosion and ruts are difficult to repair. A third issue is safety. Anglers parking along the headquarters road would need to make their way across about 30 feet of slippery boulders to reach the waters edge. Injuries are inevitable. During the winter, these boulders are usually snow-covered, providing a good ramp down to the ice. Once on the ice, there is no need to hop from boulder to boulder like there is during the summer. Fourth, shoreline fishing would conflict with birders who use the headquarters road for this activity, and because fishing would likely scare the birds away from the area. Lastly, there are literally hundreds of good fishing lakes in northeastern South Dakota.

Because fishing and other recreational activities can disturb waterfowl, the Service has determined that boating and spring and summer fishing activities on Waubay NWR would interfere with breeding and migratory birds and is not compatible with Refuge purposes.

Objective
R4.2 Provide unique ice fishing opportunities during daylight hours and without the use of vehicles, including snowmobiles, on Refuge lakes from the end of deer firearm seasons (early December) to ice-out.

Rationale for Objective: Wildlife use of the Refuge is more limited in winter months. Since there are fewer direct impacts with wildlife, especially waterfowl, ice-fishing is deemed compatible with Refuge purposes. Limiting ice fishing to day-use only and not allowing vehicles (including snowmobiles) on the ice reduces disturbances to wintering deer. It also provides a unique experience for the user; one that is not marred by the view of numerous vehicles, permanent ice shacks, or excessive noise. This helps to preserve the wild and peaceful nature of the Refuge setting.

The current fishery is opportunistic due to current water conditions, as explained above. No efforts will be made to sustain this fishery on the Refuge once water levels begin to decline. Spring and Hillebrand Lake will eventually separate from Waubay Lake and each other at some time. When this occurs, shallow waters and winterkill will, again, likely prohibit a viable fishery on the Refuge. The Service will not take means, such as fish stocking and storing water to keep lake levels high, to maintain the fishery.

Strategies:
■ Maintain ban on vehicles, overnight shacks, and night fishing.
■ Continue use of "Youth Ice Fishing Day" to teach methods and ethics of ice fishing to area children.
■ Work with South Dakota Game, Fish and Parks to conduct law enforcement patrols to ensure regulation compliance and to provide a safe experience for all visitors.
■ Identify areas open to fishing and inform the public about Refuge fishing regulations and access through signs, news releases, and pamphlets.

Environmental Education

Environmental education programs are offered on a case-by-case basis, when requested and if staff are available. This often limits the number of groups that can be accommodated. A new program called "1-2-3 To The Refuge" was developed in 2001 to bring all first, second, and third graders in Day County to the Refuge to learn about a variety of environmental subjects. It is hoped this program will be expanded to include other counties in the District as well.

Objective

R4.3 Improve the environmental education program by doubling the number of students reached on the Refuge from 300 to 600 in the next 5 years.

Rationale for Objective: Although the Refuge is within 30 miles of six schools, few educators take advantage of the resources the Refuge has to offer. Oftentimes, teachers do not feel they have enough information to lead an educational program. Developing and implementing educational programs that may be used with or without refuge staff assistance may encourage more teachers to use the Refuge for science and environmental based curricula.

Strategies:
- Develop educational packets about Refuge habitats that can be used by educators during Refuge field trips with minimal staff assistance.
- Conduct one teacher workshop, annually, to prepare them to lead environmental education programs for their students.
- Seek partners and explore development of an environmental education center for programs and student research, either on the Refuge or nearby.
- Continue development of "1-2-3 To The Refuge" to include 43 schools in the six county area and reach a wider audience of first, second, and third grade students.
- Conduct or host as least 10 schools and group tours on the Refuge per year.

Wildlife Observation, Wildlife Photography, Interpretation, and Community Involvement

The Refuge has a number of trails, signs, exhibits, and other visitor use facilities. Some are adequate, but most could use some updating or expanding to improve visitor experiences and Service messages. Currently, interpretive kiosks with leaflet dispensers are located at Headquarters and the Observation Tower. Although these are good locations, visitors must drive 1.5 miles into the Refuge before finding them. Providing an orientation kiosk near the entrance would greatly improve visitor orientation to Refuge lands. Interpretive panels for the existing kiosks were developed in the 1980s or earlier. Many have outdated information and do not reflect current Service messages or standards. Oftentimes, these are the only messages the public sees, especially during weekends when the office is closed. These panels need to be updated to better educate the public about current issues or problems.

Many visitors come to the refuge hoping to get out of their cars and do some exploring. Two walking trails are available during daylight hours. One is about ½ mile long and is located near the Headquarters building. A portion of this trail is accessible to persons with disabilities. The other trail travels approximately ¼ mile up a small hill to a view of Spring Lake and native prairie. Both trails include interpretive signs. Possible locations for longer trails include Headquarters Island to the west, West Woods (when water levels recede), and/or a grassland trail on the east side of the Refuge. The Headquarters Island also offers the opportunity to develop a short boardwalk and viewing/photography blind near a wetland with wonderful wildlife viewing potential.

Another potential trail site should be considered in the long-term future. Day County 3A is a north-south county road which cut across the western edge of the Refuge. Currently, this road is completely inundated within Refuge boundaries. When water levels recede - which may take 10 to 15 years - Refuge staff would consult with Day County officials to ask them to consider not reconstructing this gravel road, but to use it as a biking, hiking, or unimproved auto tour route. This would help to retain the remote and wild nature of the Refuge and could increase tourism by offering unique opportunities for wildlife observation and wildlife photography.

Half of the Headquarters building is used for office space, the other half for visitor use and interpretation. Even with movable exhibits, this space begins to feel quite crowded with 20 to 30 people. This limits the ability to present programs, or host open houses or meetings where more than 30 people are expected. Staff generally make use of facilities off-Refuge for events that draw larger crowds, but this is inconvenient when staff would like to use the Refuge for part of the program or allow visitors to explore the Refuge after the program. Constructing additional space for public presentations, meetings, and interpretive programs would give staff more flexibility when developing or hosting such events.

Objectives

R4.4 Expand and improve Refuge access, programs, and public use facilities to better accommodate visitors of all abilities and ages in their use of the Refuge, increasing potential for use by 5,000 people, within 7 years.

Rationale for Objective: While a variety of visitor facilities currently exist at the Refuge, the value and quality of the visitor experience could be improved through the development of additional facilities planned utilizing universal design principles which allow access by visitors of all ages and abilities. In addition, many facilities and signs need to be updated to present a better image of the Service to the public and enhance their visit to the Refuge.

Strategies:
- Develop a kiosk near the Refuge entrance to provide visitor information and orientation to Refuge lands.
- Update existing kiosk interpretive panels to reflect current Service messages and standards as advised in the 2001 Visitor Services Requirement report prepared by the regional Education and Visitor Services group.
- Develop one or two longer hiking trails with an observation blind to provide more opportunities to experience Refuge habitats and wildlife. Make part or all of these trails accessible to people with disabilities.
- Explore development of a low impact trail system (walking, biking, or unimproved auto tour route) on Day County 3A (currently inundated) in conjunction with Day County officials to offer additional wildlife observation opportunities.
- Construct additional space at headquarters to be used for public presentations, meetings, and other interpretive programs.
- Ensure all new visitor materials and facilities reach the broadest audience possible by following the Universal Design concept.

R4.5 Develop 5 public outreach programs to foster public appreciation for the resources of the Refuge to gain support from individuals and groups that can help the Refuge achieve its goals.

Rationale for Objective: In order to achieve many of the Refuge's goals, community support and involvement are needed. Getting local communities and people involved in Refuge goals promotes a sense of ownership, and local communities often benefit from the increase in tourism . Currently, one or two special events are offered each year, usually National Wildlife Refuge Week and the Christmas Bird Count. Presenting additional programs throughout the year will help to bring visitors to the Refuge and foster a greater appreciation for the resources Refuges have to offer, especially for public use and education.

Strategies:
- Develop a Refuge Friends Group within 5 years.
- Involve tourist boards and Chambers of Commerce in program development and promotion.
- Develop and implement at least four special events annually, such as National Wildlife Refuge Week, National Wildlife Week, Migratory Bird Day, National Fishing Day, Christmas Bird Count, bird-watching events, etc.
- Inform local wildlife and community groups once a year about the importance and economic benefits of the Refuge, Refuge activities, management, and issues.
- Visit with congressional offices annually to keep them up-to-date on Refuge activities, management, and issues.
- Maintain a Waubay Complex website with current information.
- Host a Refuge Open House every year.
- Write 10 news releases for local and state newspapers annually. Conduct television and radio spots upon request.

R4.6 Within 5 years, develop and promote an active volunteer program to recruit 20 volunteers contributing 500 hours per year to enhance the Refuge's ability to meet goals and objectives.

Rationale for Objective: Many opportunities to promote the Refuge are missed because of a lack of dollars or staff. An active volunteer program can help recoup these missed opportunities and turn them into achievements. Developing and promoting an active volunteer program would help accomplish some of these goals without the need to hire additional staff. It would also help build local support for the Refuge as volunteers share their positive experiences with others in the community.

Strategies:
- Develop a Refuge Friends group to help organize and recruit volunteers.
- Work with the South Dakota Volunteer Coordinator to develop a volunteer program to meet Refuge needs.
- Provide room and board for volunteers while they are working on the Complex.
- Develop two trailer pads for volunteer use.

Waubay Wetland Management District

The Service has varying amounts of influence on lands within the Wetland Management District (WMD). These lands include Waterfowl Production Areas (WPA); grassland, wetland, and conservation easements; and private lands. WPAs are owned in fee-title and can be directly manipulated to provide high quality wetlands and nesting cover primarily for waterfowl and other migratory birds; however, many other wildlife species also benefit from these areas. The various easement programs provide protection for their respective habitats but ownership and management ultimately rests with the landowner. The Partners for Fish and Wildlife Program was developed specifically to provide technical assistance and often cash incentives for landowners eager to improve their own lands. WMD goals seek to address the land on a landscape level while working within the constraints of these differing landownership (and management) classes.

Habitat loss and degradation are often the biggest threats facing many wildlife species, including waterfowl and other grassland-dependent birds. Therefore, the primary focus of management on the WMD is providing quality habitat through preservation, restoration, and enhancement. This is the most effective and efficient way to manage Service lands for the benefit of wildlife. Specific wildlife population objectives have not been developed since populations are affected by many variables outside of Service control, such as weather, disease, and pollution.

Habitat

- *D1 - Habitat Goal: To preserve, restore, and enhance the ecological diversity of grasslands, wetlands, and native woodlands of the Prairie Pothole Region of the Great Plains on the Waubay Wetland Management District.*

Grasslands

The Great Plains of North America once covered over a million square miles through the center of the continent. Tallgrass prairie comprised the eastern third of this vast ecosystem, covering almost 200 million acres. An extraordinary biodiversity developed from complex interactions between animals, soils, plants, climate, and fire. The loss of natural disturbances, fragmentation, and increased invasion of nonnative species has rendered the tallgrass prairie region one of North America's most endangered ecosystems (Noss et al. 1995).

The six counties of northeastern South Dakota encompasses 3.4 million acres, half of which has been converted to cropland. Of the 1.3 million acres of remaining grasslands, approximately one million acres is considered native prairie. This "native" prairie is defined as grassland that has never been plowed, but all plant communities have been altered from pristine conditions, to some extent, due to nonnative plant introductions, livestock grazing impacts, lack of fire, and other factors since European settlement. It is safe to assume that few, if any, native grasslands retain the species composition, number of species, or structure of the original grasslands encountered only 150 years ago. Even so, there are at least 300 species of plants, 113 species of butterflies, 35 species of reptiles and amphibians, 60 species of mammals, and 260 species of birds known to breed in or use tallgrass prairie in North and South Dakota (USFWS 2000).

The following objectives work together to make an effect on a landscape scale - to stem the loss of grasslands to reduce fragmentation, protect remaining tallgrass prairie, and restore some of the lost natural ecosystem processes and biodiversity.

Grassland Preservation Objectives

D1.1 Preserve, on average, 10,000 acres of grasslands annually for the benefit of waterfowl and other grassland-dependent wildlife.

Rationale for Objective: Today, less than 4 percent of the original tallgrass prairie remains (Steinauer and Collins 1996). As the average prairie size has diminished from 1,000,000 acres in 1790 to today's 40 acres, biodiversity has been reduced (Apfelbaum and Chapman 1996). These smaller, isolated tracts are less complex and, therefore, less able to renew themselves or respond to changes in the environment. These grasslands continue to disappear. USDA data compiled by the USFWS showed that 700,000 acres of native prairie in South Dakota were converted to crop production from 1985 to 1995 (C. Madsen, pers. comm.). More recently, the Farm Services Agency in South Dakota reported that 40,000 acres of native prairie had been plowed under for crops in 2001. At the same time, grassland-dependent bird species across the continent have shown the most consistent and widespread declines of all migratory birds (Knopf 1994). Butterflies and other invertebrates have also suffered: there are seven butterfly species of concern that occur in South Dakota (Moffat and McPhillips 1993).

This objective seeks to stem the continued losses of grasslands and associated species by purchasing grassland easements from willing sellers and with minimal fee-title purchases. This objective cannot stop the continued conversion of grasslands but can protect what is still there. Since less than 3 percent of the land base in Waubay WMD is devoted to wildlife management, protecting private lands becomes paramount to restoring the overall health of grasslands and wildlife populations. Keeping land in grass cover will also help to reduce soil erosion, improve water quality, and help trap snow and rain, recharging water supplies.

Purchasing easements from willing sellers is the preferred method to protect against further loss of habitat in the six northeast counties. Ten thousand acres per year is an achievable goal although this may fall short if conversion rates continue at present levels. Easements will be selected and evaluated by tract size, percent native prairie, number of waterfowl pairs it supports, and other factors (Appendix J). Occasionally it may be advantageous to purchase a tract under fee-title to gain more control over the management and other rights. Fee-title purchases from willing sellers will be considered only for larger acreages (160 acres or greater) of exceptional habitat. Larger blocks of grassland (40 acres or greater) have been found to attract more nesting waterfowl, with increased nest success (Duebbert et al. 1981). In addition, the species richness of grassland birds is positively associated with the size of a grassland area (Herkert 1994).

Strategies:
- In easement procurement, focus on areas scoring 40 or more pairs/square mile on the Waterfowl Breeding Pair Distribution (WBPD) (Map 8) for the benefit of waterfowl and migratory birds.
- Focus on tracts exceeding threshold scores for the grassland easement evaluation worksheet. Factors evaluated include tract size, percentage of native prairie, soil capability, etc. (Appendix J).
- Enforce contract terms on all grassland easements through annual monitoring, and send reminder letters every 3 to 5 years to contract owners.
- Develop a Region-wide computerized mapping system of grassland easements, with the lead of the Habitat and Population Evaluation Team (HAPET) and the Realty Division, to greatly reduce staff time and errors on manual mapping and facilitate information transfer to other agencies and individuals.
- Consider potential or likely ranges where remote populations of the western prairie fringed orchid might occur.
- Inform easement holders of the Partners for Fish and Wildlife program that provides technical assistance to private landowners on rotational grazing systems to provide more residual vegetation for waterfowl and other ground-nesting birds.
- Preserve unique grassland/wetland complexes by making limited (less than 500 acres annually) fee-title purchases, using Duck Stamp funds.

D1.2 Work with the Dakota Tallgrass Prairie Wildlife Management Area ˉ staff to protect 100,000 acres of high-quality tallgrass prairie in eastern South Dakota, by 2016, to ensure the future of this highly endangered ecosystem.

Rationale for Objective: The Dakota Tallgrass Prairie Wildlife Management Area seeks to preserve a total of 190,000 acres of native tallgrass prairie in eastern North and South Dakota to help maintain biodiversity and slow habitat fragmentation (USFWS 2000). Efforts will be made to cluster protected areas into 10,000 to 20,000 acre blocks. Lands will be preserved primarily through perpetual easements purchased from willing sellers.

Nearly all of the original tallgrass prairie has been lost to agriculture and other development (Noss et al. 1995). What remains, tends to be in isolated parcels, surrounded by agricultural lands. This isolation and small patch size exacerbate edge effects, pesticide and contaminant drift, infiltration of exotic species, and increases the susceptibility of prairie-dependent species to extirpation or extinction (Steinauer and Collins 1996, The Nature Conservancy 1998). Some of the largest remaining tracts of native tallgrass prairie occur on the Coteau (Leoschke 1997). This is largely due to the hilly and rocky nature of the region which lends itself more to grazing than crop production. This makes this part of northeastern South Dakota essential to the preservation of the tallgrass prairie ecosystem. This objective recognizes that Waubay WMD can play a large part in fulfilling the goals of the Dakota Tallgrass Prairie Project.

Strategies:
- Assist Aberdeen Wetland Acquisition office and Dakota Tallgrass Prairie Wildlife Management Area coordinator to locate and contact prospective easement holders.
- Recruit farm organizations, USDA, conservation groups, and others to promote grassland preservation programs.
- Assist with development and use of a Geographic Information System (GIS) mapping method to aid identification and delineation of native prairie tracts.
- Acquire a 300+ acre high quality (diverse native vegetation composition) tallgrass prairie tract, fee-title, for the perpetuation of prairie species and grassland-dependent birds. This tract could also serve as a seed source for future restorations and as a demonstration site for private, State and Federal agencies to promote current management programs and techniques.
- Cluster protected areas into 10,000 to 20,000 acre blocks.
- Develop funding sources and programs outside the Small Wetlands Acquisition Program for tallgrass prairie that often is not associated with adjacent wetlands in the Minnesota-Red River Lowlands, Lake Dakota Plain, and the James River Lowland.

D1.3 Work with partners to develop a 20,000+ acre Prairie Coteau Natural Area in southwestern Roberts County or southeastern Marshall County to protect northern tallgrass prairie habitat and to educate the public about this dynamic and rich ecosystem.

Rationale for Objective: Few people have seen an intact piece of prairie ecosystem or are aware of the complexities and interactions that make up a healthy system. The development of a large tract of prairie could be enhanced and used as a showcase for tourism, for educating landowners and school children, and as a center for research. Benefits to the landscape would include increased air and water quality, greater biodiversity, reduced soil erosion and fragmentation of habitat.

Strategies:
- Assist The Nature Conservancy (TNC) or other partners to fulfill their plan to acquire this habitat with a combination of private, State, or Federal funding.
- Assist partners with developing a land management system using grazing impacts and fire as a demonstration area for land managers on the Prairie Coteau.
- Assist partners in developing a showcase for natural prairie system to be used by the area's educators.
- Stress natural disturbance regimes, research, and environmental education programs in management of the Natural Area to benefit all preservation, restoration, and enhancement efforts for prairie on the Prairie Coteau.

Grassland Restoration and Enhancement Objectives

D1.4 Convert cropland and poor quality tame grass to diverse grasslands, emphasizing native plants, on 295,500 acres of private land and 4,500 acres of Waterfowl Production Areas, for a total of 300,000 acres, within 15 years.

Rationale for Objective: Changes made to private lands have a greater impact overall on the landscape than the smaller number of acres in public ownership (less than 3 percent of lands in the WMD are state or federally protected). Bird use and productivity are negatively influenced by cultivated lands. Despite its high availability in some areas, cropland is the least preferred nesting habitat for ducks except northern pintails (Naugle et al. 2000). Nongame bird species may also be negatively impacted by the presence of tame grasses (Wilson and Belcher 1989). Through the Partners for Fish and Wildlife and USDA programs, thousands of acres of lands could be converted to native grasses, thus stemming the continued losses of grasslands and restoring poor quality tame grasslands and croplands to higher quality native seedings. This may also ultimately help reduce global warming effects as prairie grasslands are superior carbon sinks (Seastedt and Knapp 1993).

Legumes currently used, usually alfalfa, mature about June 1; pushing this date back to August 1 would save many nesting birds. Current haying practices on private haylands involve two or three cuttings, the first usually occurring in June during the height of the nesting season. This can cause much damage to nests and is oftentimes fatal to incubating females. Native vetches can be used as an alternative to alfalfa. Canada milkvetch matures later so there is no loss of protein if cutting is delayed until after the nesting season. The addition of native forbs, such as Canada milkvetch, may assist butterfly populations by providing a nectar source during flight periods.

Strategies:
- Inventory and map existing croplands and tame grasses on the WMD within one year.
- Research appropriate native seed mixes and their availability, within one year.
- Provide technical and personnel assistance to USDA and other agencies implementing private land wildlife habitat programs such as Conservation Reserve Program (CRP), Wetland Reserve Program (WRP), Waterbank, and other set-aside programs.
- Provide financial incentives and technical assistance for landowners to reseed their croplands and low quality grasslands to native prairie communities.
- Convert croplands on acquired grassland easement properties and WPAs to native prairie communities.
- Convert 300 acres of WPA tame grasslands to native plant communities, annually.
- Manage restored native plantings on WPAs for maximum height and density, based on grass species involved and site conditions.
- Develop management plans on WPAs to monitor restored native grasslands for weeds, grassland condition, and wildlife response.
- Restore all WPA food plots to grasslands within 2 years.
- Manage tame grasslands on WPAs not scheduled for conversion to natives for maximum height and density, based on grass species involved and site conditions. Ideally, residual cover in mid-April would measure at least 20 cm (8 inches) total visual obstruction (as measured by a Robel pole) for waterfowl nesting (Duebbert et al. 1981).
- Work with partners to develop three sites demonstrating late-maturing legumes as a hay crop.

D1.5 Assist Partners for Fish and Wildlife to enhance grasslands on approximately 5,000 acres of private lands, annually, for a total of 75,000 acres.

Rationale for Objective: In northeastern South Dakota, most landowners practice season long grazing, often using the same pasture year-after-year, with no rest. Native vegetation is altered, resulting in plant species better adapted to repeated clipping or those of low stature. Certain plant species increase under these conditions while others decrease or disappear altogether. In addition, pastures grazed season long often exhibit less residual cover and higher rates of erosion than idled pastures or those under rotational systems. This type of grazing tends to have negative effects on the production of most upland nesting birds (Kirsch et al. 1978) as well as limiting maximum livestock production. The weight of beef produced per unit area can increase by 15 to 44 percent by changing to a short duration or twice-over rotation system (Hertel 1987). Monitoring of these systems can help make sure objectives for both wildlife and beef production are being met.

An evaluation of grazing systems by Barker et al. 1990 in North Dakota found that systems designed to leave more residual vegetation were more attractive and productive for nesting ducks than traditional season-long grazing systems. Their study found ducks used well managed pastures at 70 percent of the rate of idled grasslands (no grazing). Since nearly 1,000,000 acres of native tallgrass prairie remains in eastern South Dakota, mostly in Waubay WMD (Higgins et al. 2001), compared to the 40,000 acres in Service ownership, the potential impact realized by improving pastured grasslands for waterfowl and other grassland birds is clear.

Strategies:
- Provide financial and technical assistance to landowners to improve wildlife habitat on existing livestock pastures.
- Provide landowners information about the use of fire to improve wildlife habitat on livestock pastures.
- Preserve and enhance grasslands by creating small wetlands (embankment ponds) that allow farmers and ranchers to maintain their current land base in its grassland status.
- Design grazing systems that leave at least 15 cm (6 inches) of vegetative cover (visual obstruction reading) on or about June 1, during the prime nesting season.
- Monitor a subset of 10 grazing systems to determine height/density of grasslands and evaluate effectiveness of the program.
- Develop new and current partnerships (conservation districts, grazing associations, agricultural groups, etc.) to promote and monitor improved grazing practices on private land.

D1.6 Eliminate 90 percent of Russian olive and juniper stands and 45 percent of other nonnative plants, such as leafy spurge and Canada thistle, on WPAs over the next 15 years.

Rationale for Objective: In the absence of regular fire, brushy and woody species can encroach on grasslands, reducing habitat for species that depend on areas free of this type of vegetation. For grassland-obligate species, woody vegetation should cover less than 5 percent of available habitat (Sample and Mossman 1997). Junipers, Russian olives, and other woody vegetation (especially that over 1m, or 39 inches, in height) in grasslands can provide habitat for nest parasites, predators, and corridors for predator movement (Berkey et al. 1993). Removing woody vegetation can improve nesting habitat and success for waterfowl and other grassland species.

Noxious weeds, particularly Canada thistle and leafy spurge, have no natural controls and can aggressively invade grasslands. This can reduce the overall biodiversity, structure, and productivity necessary for healthy grasslands and wildlife species. Integrated Pest Management (IPM) is a multi-faceted approach to nonnative plant control that uses a practical, economical, and scientifically based combination of biological, mechanical, and chemical control methods. Oftentimes, a combination of methods is used for the most effective treatment. Promising results have been seen in the reduction of leafy spurge using biological controls, particularly *Apthona spp.* (flea beetles). USFWS will continue to urge the use of bio-controls to reduce the use of potentially harmful chemicals in the environment. Bio-control methods can also reduce landowner costs and time spent spraying chemicals.

Strategies:
- Inventory and map existing distribution of nonnative plants on WPAs within 10 years.
- Utilize a combination of biological, chemical and mechanical means, with an emphasis on biological control (especially in native grasslands) to reduce noxious weed infestations and protect biodiversity.
- Conduct annual flea beetle collections and distribute to infected areas on public and private lands to control leafy spurge.
- Promote biological noxious weed (Canada thistle, absinthe wormwood) control methods on private lands by providing insectories on Federal lands, education, and assistance to state biological control groups and landowners.

D1.7 Over the next 10 years, develop a Habitat Management Plan for the 61 Category "A" WPAs to maintain maximum vegetative cover during Spring of each year to provide waterfowl nesting cover for blue-winged teals, mallards, and gadwalls.

Rationale for Objective: Some WPAs are small and relatively unmanageable (i.e., are all water or inaccessible). Other sites have recently become unmanageable due to high water levels. In an average year and with current dollars and staff, 10 to 15 percent of uplands are managed in some form. An Integrated Habitat Management Plan will prioritize WPAs, allowing managers to better direct their time and energies to the best tracts (or those most needing management), thereby improving or maintaining what will generally be larger tracts capable of sustaining greater diversity and wildlife populations. As each WPA varies in habitat, size, landscape location, developments, or management tools that can be used, developing individual site plans will help current and future managers know what the site has for resources, problems, cooperators, past management, which management tools worked, and which did not work.

Strategies:

- Determine the level of management intensity on each WPA using the WPA Priority Management list (Appendix H).
- Develop individual WPA unit plans, based on the Priority Management List, with objectives and strategies for management, biological inventories, and monitoring activities carried out on each site. Site plans would determine current grassland condition and strive toward optimum potential condition.
- Establish monitoring criteria to evaluate grassland management techniques on WPAs, within 5 years.
- Develop prescribed burn plans for all WPAs which would benefit from periodic burning.
- Develop site plans for all existing water control structures on WPAs.
- Develop plans to incorporate mechanical (haying, mowing, cropping, cutting), chemical, biological, and grazing weed control techniques into WPA management.
- Decrease the number of Category "C" WPAs (see Appendix H) by creating five larger blocks of contiguous lands using land exchanges with South Dakota Game, Fish and Parks, private landowners, and others.

Wetlands

Wetlands are lands where saturation with water is the dominant factor determining the nature of soil development and the types of plant and animal communities living in the soil and on its surface (Cowardin et al. 1979). It is estimated that the contiguous United States once contained 221 million acres of wetlands, just 200 years ago (Dahl 1990). By the mid-1970s, only 46 percent of the original acreage remained (Tiner 1984). Wetlands now cover about 5 percent of the landscape of the lower 48 states. One of the most productive wetland regions in the world is the Prairie Pothole Region. Containing only 10 percent of the breeding habitat in North America, this region produces up to 50 percent of the continent's waterfowl (Batt et al. 1989). It is estimated that over 19 million acres of potholes (wetlands) were once present in the Prairie Pothole Region, sometimes covering as much as 40 to 60 percent of the landscape (Frayer et al. 1983). Currently, only about 35 percent of the original prairie potholes remain (USDOI 1988).

Objectives

D1.8 Preserve, on average, 2,000 acres of wetlands annually for the benefit of waterfowl and other migratory birds.

> Rationale for Objective: The average size of wetlands in eastern South Dakota is only .4 acre; 72.9 percent of wetlands are #1 acre and 92.1 percent are #5 (Johnson and Higgins 1997). The small size and temporary nature of many wetlands in South Dakota makes them prime targets for drainage. Approximately 35 percent of South Dakota's wetlands have been destroyed since settlement, most in the last 60 years (Johnson and Higgins 1997). In 1981, Weller believed that all privately owned prairie wetlands in the United States would be drained by 2050. Hundreds of species of fish, wildlife, and plants inhabit or use wetlands during some part of their life cycle. More than 50 percent of the Nation's migratory bird species use wetlands for nesting, migration, and wintering (USFWS 1990). About one-third of federally threatened or endangered species require wetland habitats for their survival. These relatively rare and critical ecosystems help protect the quality of our waters by reducing sediments and erosion, and storing nutrients (Kusler and Brooks 1987, Mitsch and Gosselink 1986). Wetlands also provide flood control and recharge groundwater supplies. Wetlands would be protected primarily through purchase of easements from willing sellers, with only rare fee-title purchases made for exceptional wetlands or wetland complexes in imminent threat of drainage.

Strategies:

- For wetland easements purchased with Duck Stamp funds, focus on areas ranking 40 pairs/square mile or better on the Waterfowl Breeding Pair Distribution (WBPD) map and on tracts meeting criteria established for the Small Wetlands Acquisition Program, including wetland complex size, presence of brood water, and other factors important for breeding waterfowl and migratory birds.
- Assist Aberdeen Wetlands Acquisition office to locate and contact prospective wetland easement sellers.
- Work with farm organizations, USDA, conservation groups, and others to promote wetland preservation programs.
- Assist USDA with their farm program wetland protection provisions and wetland easement programs.
- Develop a computerized mapping system of protected wetlands, with the lead of Habitat and Population Evaluation Team (HAPET) and the Realty Division.
- Map all wetlands on pre-1976 wetland easement contracts.
- Enforce contract terms on all wetland easements through annual inspections, and send reminder letters every 3 to 5 years to contract owners of wetland easements.

D1.9 Work with Partners for Fish and Wildlife to restore a minimum of 1,000 wetland acres annually on private lands, for a total of 15,000 acres over 15 years.

Rationale for Objective: Since settlement, 35 percent of South Dakota's wetlands have been destroyed, most in the last 60 years (Johnson and Higgins 1997). Since small wetlands are easier to drain than larger ones, the biggest impacts of drainage affect the temporary and seasonal wetlands most important for breeding and feeding waterfowl (Baldassarre and Bolen 1994). To reduce the effects of continued wetland drainage and restore previously drained wetlands, this plan would work with private landowners, federal, state and local governments, and private organizations to promote and provide assistance for wetland restoration. Restored wetlands may or may not be protected by a Service wetland easement.

Strategies:
- Partner with private organizations, landowners, watershed groups, State and other Federal agencies, Conservation Districts, and other partners to restore wetlands.
- Provide technical and personnel assistance to USDA and other agencies implementing private land wildlife habitat programs such as CRP, WRP, Waterbank, and other set-aside programs.
- Restore 100 percent of wetlands on WPAs and newly acquired easement lands, within 2 years of acquisition.

Watersheds

A watershed is the area of land that catches rain or snow and drains or seeps into a marsh, stream, river, lake, or groundwater. What happens on the land in a watershed will ultimately affect the water. A lake that is surrounded by cropland or feedlots will suffer from increased sediment and phosphorous loads, reducing water clarity and increasing algal blooms and eutrophication (SD State Lakes Preservation Committee 1977). Lake cabins and associated sewage treatment needs can also have drastic effects on water quality.

Objective

D1.10 Participate in watershed protection projects throughout the WMD to implement conservation practices to enhance wildlife habitat and water quality over the next 15 years.

Rationale for Objective: The State of South Dakota has an active program for watershed improvement in which conservation practices are applied to individual watersheds over a set period of time, usually 5 years. Funding and personnel are concentrated on an individual watershed, then the process is repeated in another watershed. Watershed conservation practices, such as improved grazing systems, conversion of cropland to grassland, wetland restoration, and wetland creation, often compliment Partners for Fish and Wildlife habitat improvement programs. Watershed protection projects concentrate on conservation practices that improve water quality, which often produces a side benefit of improving habitat conditions for wildlife and fish. Funding packages often can be developed to partner local funds with matching federal dollars to maximize the acres impacted by wildlife habitat improvement projects. Watershed protection groups currently active in the WMD and working with the Service Partners for Fish and Wildlife program include Big Stone Lake, Pickerel Lake, Blue Dog Lake, Upper Waubay Lake, Upper Big Sioux River, Little Minnesota River, North Fork Whetstone River, Pelican Lake, Lake Byron, Crow Creek, Wild Rice River, White Lake, and Clear Lake Watershed Protection Projects.

Strategies:
- Research current water quality in Bitter and Waubay Lakes to establish a baseline for future comparisons.
- Develop partnerships with The Nature Conservancy, South Dakota Game, Fish and Parks, local governments, private landowners, and others.
- Continue implementing Natural Resource Conservation Service (NRCS) best management practices on Service lands.
- Cooperate with Waubay Watershed Protection Project (WWPP) to take water quality samples and monitor annually.
- Assist watershed protection projects through Partners for Fish and Wildlife efforts to implement conservation practices on private lands (e.g. buffer/filter strips, fencing cattle off riparian areas, wetland restoration, rotational grazing systems, restoring grasslands).
- Assist Partners for Fish and Wildlife program and other watershed partners with monitoring compliance of conservation practices.
- Purchase grassland and wetland easements to reduce sedimentation and nutrient loading.

Native Woodlands

Native woodlands are a natural part of the landscape, occurring in the draws on the east slopes of the Coteau des Prairie and also at the edges of larger lakes and lake systems. Most, if not all, of the Prairie Coteau woodlands (including the Sica Hollow area), were cut for lumber, fenceposts, and firewood by the early part of the 20th century for use by Fort Sisseton and the influx of settlers in 1892 (Leoschke 1997). Present day woodlands have regrown from that era.

No long-term studies of avian communities have been conducted in wooded draws. Casual observations have found five species of warblers during spring migration as well as reports of turkey vultures and pileated woodpeckers in wooded coulees in Roberts County. One study of woodland types in the Little Missouri National Grasslands found that certain neotropical migrants (red-eyed vireo, black-and-white warbler, yellow-breasted chat, American redstart, lazuli bunting, rufous-sided towhee, lark sparrow, and American goldfinch) were significantly more abundant in ash woodlands than in juniper, pine or even cottonwood habitats (Hopkins et al. 1986).

Objective

D1.11 Preserve 1,000 acres of critical blocks of native woodlands on the Wetland Management District, by year 2017.

> Rationale for Objective: Although these habitats cover less than 1 percent of the northern Great Plains, wooded draws can attract a disproportionately rich number of bird species compared to other plains habitats (Dobkin 1992). These woodlands are often subjected to heavy grazing (Faanes 1987) and/or used for lumber and firewood. Cattle grazing of wooded draws can create open canopy stands that consist of a low shrub layer, a sparse overstory of decadent trees, an herbaceous layer of invasive, mostly alien species, and the complete absence of intermediate layers (Hodorff et al. 1988). Grazing will often preclude any woody plant recruitment by trees and tall shrubs, leading to the eventual conversion of these woodlands to grass-forb communities. Preserving and understanding these woodland habitats may be vital to certain migratory and breeding birds.

> Strategies:
> - Inventory and map native woodland habitat base.
> - Establish baseline bird inventory of woodland habitats.
> - Document use of and threats to native woodlands for breeding and migratory birds and other wildlife.
> - Develop a task force with South Dakota Game, Fish and Parks; The Nature Conservancy; Audubon Society; Sisseton-Wahpeton Sioux Tribe; Coteau Watch; and others to identify priority woodlands for preservation.
> - Protect native woodlands through easements or fee-title purchases from willing sellers.

Wildlife

- *D2 - Wildlife Goal: To promote a natural diversity and abundance of native flora and fauna of the Prairie Pothole Region of the Great Plains on Waubay Wetland Management District.*

Since wildlife populations are dynamic and can be affected by factors such as weather, disease, pollution or other factors outside of Service control, specific wildlife population objectives have not been developed. It is especially impossible to develop specific wildlife population objectives for a wetland management district with hundreds of disjunct pieces of land spread throughout a wide range of habitats, land use, and even physiographic regions. Therefore, the following objectives focus primarily on increasing our knowledge of wildlife needs and monitoring wildlife populations and land use patterns in order to better direct habitat management. Particular efforts are made in the arenas of migratory birds, such as waterfowl and other grassland-dependent species; federally listed threatened and endangered species; and state species at risk.

Objectives

D2.1 Within the 15 year life of this plan, conserve habitat capable of supporting 500,000 breeding ducks that achieve a recruitment rate of 0.6 under average environmental conditions, with all Waterfowl Production Areas achieving a minimum recruitment rate of 0.49.

> Rationale for Objective: This is a step-down objective from the U.S. Prairie Pothole Joint Venture (PPJV) Implementation Plan. The PPJV itself is a step-down plan from the North American Waterfowl Management Plan. Both plans focus on protecting, restoring, and enhancing wetlands and grasslands in order to achieve waterfowl population objectives. Accordingly, this CCP also focuses on providing quality habitat for waterfowl.

> Strategies:
> - Preserve, restore, and enhance wetland and grassland habitat as outlined in objectives D1.1, D1.4, D1.5, D1.7, D1.8, and D1.9.

D2.2 Develop a Monitoring Plan, within 3 years, to locate and track specific locations used by the following endangered or threatened species: bald eagle, piping plover, whooping crane, Eskimo curlew, interior least tern, American burying beetle, Topeka shiner, and western prairie fringed orchid.

> Rationale for Objective: The species listed above may potentially be found on or use WPAs for some part of their life-cycle. Confirming their presence and location will help Refuge managers prevent potential adverse effects from some management actions, such as prescribed burning and pesticide application.

> Strategies:
> - Investigate and document sightings and reports of bald eagle nests.
> - Promote protection and perpetuation of native fisheries, including Topeka shiner, by working with partners to protect streams, lakes, and watersheds.
> - Protect sites on the WMD used by endangered and threatened species.
> - Use appropriate management techniques and timing to help ensure continued survival of these species.

D2.3 Develop a Monitoring Plan, within 3 years, to locate and track specific locations used by the following State species at risk: regal fritillary, Dakota skipper, and powesheik skipper butterflies; osprey; banded killifish; central mudminnow; trout-perch; northern redbelly dace; northern redbelly snake.

Rationale for Objective: South Dakota's endangered species law was passed in 1977 to ensure the protection of threatened and endangered species within the State. The Game, Fish, and Parks Commission reviews the list of species every 2 years with species added or deleted depending on their vulnerability, with the Game, Fish and Parks Department in charge of the protection of listed species. The South Dakota Natural Heritage Program also documents and monitors over 400 plant and animal species considered at risk in South Dakota. Ongoing monitoring is achieved through the cooperation of various agencies and individuals and helps to keep species from declining to the point where they must be listed. We can further this goal by monitoring these species as well as limiting or adjusting habitat management efforts to reduce potential negative impacts.

Certain species may also serve as indicators of the health of an ecosystem, such as butterflies. Butterflies are part of the prairie ecosystem. If these species are in trouble, other endemic (and harder to track) species may also be in decline. Tracking these butterflies and adjusting management to benefit them should benefit other prairie endemics, improve the health of the prairie ecosystem, and help to prevent the listing of these and other species that have declined due to the poor health of prairie habitats.

Strategies:
- Initiate surveys during appropriate flight times on WPAs with native prairie habitat to monitor presence, abundance, and locations of these at risk species.
- Protect WPA sites where the above mentioned species are located.
- Use appropriate management techniques and timing to ensure continued survival of these butterflies.

D2.4 Rewrite and update the Wildlife Inventory Plan to include methodology for a variety of surveys, increasing the number and quality of surveys for residential and migratory wildlife species, within 10 years.

Rationale for Objective: This objective would seek to increase the overall knowledge of wildlife species present so that informed decisions can be made regarding habitat needs and the development of models or the use of indicator species as a method of measuring the success of management goals and practices.

Strategies:
- Conduct an additional Breeding Bird Survey route (one is currently done).
- Conduct passerine surveys on selected intensively managed WPAs to monitor for management impacts to grassland species.
- Locate sharp-tailed grouse and prairie chicken dancing and booming grounds.
- Continue 4-square mile waterfowl pair surveys at current levels (22 plots).
- Continue participation in cooperative surveys such as mourning dove, sandhill crane, Christmas Bird Count, etc.
- Cooperate with South Dakota Game, Fish and Parks on deer surveys and population management.
- Review regional and national plans to help determine how to broaden surveys, for which species.
- Research and determine appropriate survey methodologies for habitats and species targeted.

Cultural Resources

- *D3 - Cultural Resources Goal: Protect and interpret significant historic and prehistoric cultural resources associated with Waubay Wetland Management District.*

Long before Europeans arrived, various cultures and native peoples occupied the Northern Great Plains, some documented as early as 12,000 years ago (Jackson and Toom 1999). Reminders of these cultures can be found throughout the WMD in burial mounds, cultural material scatter sites (containing artifacts such as ceramics, tools, or animal bones among other things), or trails. It is important to remind ourselves of these peoples and how they lived on the land, making use of its rich resources, without causing the vast changes that Europeans have wrought on the landscape.

Objectives
D3.1 Within the 15 year life of this plan, locate, identify, map, and determine NRHP eligibility of all significant historic and prehistoric cultural and archaeological resources on 30 Category "A" WPAs.

Rationale for Objective: Although a recent study has been compiled for archaeological resources found in and around the Refuge, a similar study has not been done for the WMD. Cultural resource sites known in the WMD have usually been discovered when water development or other ground breaking projects required a survey to comply with the National Historic Preservation Act (NHPA). This is probably the best way to find and survey these culturally important sites considering the extent of the WMD and the impossibility of doing a wide-ranging study.

Strategies:
- Utilize standard law enforcement practices and strategies to protect cultural resources already identified and those that may be discovered where development of water control structures, wetland restorations, and other ground breaking activities will occur.
- Produce a cultural resource overlay for Geographic Information System (GIS) database.
- Consult with the Regional Historic Preservation Officer prior to all proposed actions.
- Avoid areas of known cultural sites and potential sensitive areas when practical, and mitigate any adverse effects to sites.
- Investigate and inventory two known archaeological resources and other possible sites, as found, for presence of cultural resources.

D3.2 Interpret the cultural resources of the WMD for visitors of all ages and abilities through a combination of 3 programs, within 7 years.

Rationale for Objective: Interpreting these sites can help to establish a link between past and present generations. Learning how other cultures lived and used natural resources can help current and future inhabitants understand their role in the environment. This insight may help to solve current issues by providing a larger backdrop and history often forgotten.

Strategies:
- Upgrade Refuge kiosk exhibit as advised in the 2001 Visitor Services Requirement report prepared by the regional Education and Visitor Services group.
- Upgrade Refuge visitor center exhibit as advised in the 2001 Visitor Services Requirement report.
- Investigate establishment of a cooperative interpretive site with Sisseton-Wahpeton Sioux Tribe.
- Ensure all new visitor materials and facilities reach the broadest audience possible by following the Universal Design concept.
- Incorporate interpretation of Wetland Management District cultural resources into the Refuge program, presenting a more comprehensive interpretive program.

Public Use and Education

■ *D4 - Wildlife-dependent Recreation Goal: To foster an understanding and appreciation of the ecology and management of the fauna and flora and of the role of humans in the Prairie Pothole Region of the Great Plains by providing Wetland Management District visitors of all abilities with compatible wildlife-dependent recreational experiences.*

The Refuge Improvement Act recognized the importance of developing an understanding and appreciation of our fish and wildlife resources and mandated six priority public uses on Refuge lands. They include hunting, fishing, wildlife observation, wildlife photography, environmental education and interpretation.

Objectives

D4.1 Continue to provide hunting, fishing, and trapping opportunities on WPAs in accordance with State regulations, seasons, and population changes.

> Rationale for Objective: When Waterfowl Production Areas are purchased, they are open to public hunting, fishing, and trapping by statute. WPAs may be opened to other recreational activities only if they do not materially interfere with or detract from the purposes for which they were established, namely to provide breeding and nesting habitat for waterfowl and other migratory birds. Travel is restricted on most WPAs to foot travel only. This helps to protect habitat and retain the wild nature of these tracts. Most of these activities also occur during fall or winter when breeding and nesting activities are done. Few improvements have been made to WPAs besides grassed parking lots and fencing to facilitate grazing management and reduce trespass problems.

> ### Strategies:
> ■ Provide law enforcement assistance to ensure compliance with State and Federal regulations on WPAs and for hunting seasons on migratory game birds.
> ■ Work with South Dakota Game, Fish and Parks to annually evaluate permit numbers, season lengths, and types.
> ■ Investigate feasibility of offering youth deer hunts or hunts for people with disabilities.

D4.2 Develop 5 educational opportunities which highlight the Wetland Management District and its role in wildlife conservation in the Prairie Pothole Region, over the next 15 years.

Rationale for Objective: Few people know about Wetland Management Districts or why they exist. Even fewer students or teachers take advantage of Waterfowl Production Areas that may be located near rural schools. This objective would actively promote environmental education opportunities and develop new programs for use either in area schools or on WPAs near schools. This would provide new opportunities for many rural schools and increase exposure of students to the environmental challenges faced today and the benefits of protecting our natural resources. Interpretive signs and a birding trail will also help reach a wider audience and increase tourism dollars and appreciation of Service programs.

Strategies:
- Conduct a minimum of one educational program at 15 schools in the WMD each year so that one-third would be served each year (there are 43 schools in the WMD).
- Develop and implement educational programs for educators to use on a WPA to explain functions of various habitats in the WMD (i.e. wetlands, prairies, and woodlands), and their importance to wildlife.
- Conduct one teacher workshop, annually, to prepare them to lead environmental education programs for their students.
- Develop at least two interpretive kiosks on WPAs located on well traveled roadways to promote and interpret the Small Wetlands Acquisition Program (possible sites: Berwald, Jensen, Grass Lake, or Lardy WPAs).
- Work with partners to develop the Coteau Birding Trail to find, map, and interpret birding hot spots to increase tourism and an appreciation of local natural resources.

V. Implementation and Monitoring

Funding and Personnel

The following staff chart shows current staff and proposed additional staffing needed to fully implement the CCP. Proposed staff increases reflect the minimum staffing plan established for the Complex. If all positions were filled, the Complex could carry out all aspects of the CCP. If some positions are not filled, all aspects of the Plan cannot be completed or those completed may be done over a longer period of time. Staffing and funding are expected to be accomplished over the 15-year life of this Plan.

Complex staff currently totals 11 positions (10.5 FTEs), plus two Private Lands biological technicians. Minimum staffing requirements would increase staffing levels to 21 positions (19 FTEs).

In fiscal year 2000, Waubay Complex had a baseline budget of $439,000 to fund annual operating expenses, including staff salaries. Station backlogs identified in fiscal year 2000 Maintenance Management System (MMS) and Refuge Operations Needs System (RONS) totaled $1,236,000 and $2,679,000, respectively. The CCP proposes to accomplish more resource protection and habitat management, which only can be realized by fully funding the MMS and RONS projects.

Current/Proposed Staffing Plan - Waubay Complex					
Position	NWR - Current	NWR - Proposed	WMD - Current	WMD - Proposed	Complex - Fully Staffed (Totals)
Project Leader GS-13	1.0				1.0
Deputy Project Leader GS-12	1.0				1.0
Wetlands Manager GS-11			0.5		0.5
Wetlands Manager GS-11				0.5	0.5
Ref. Operations Spec. GS-9			1.0		1.0
Complex Biologist GS-11	1.0				1.0
Wildlife Biologist GS-9				1.0	1.0
Resource Specialist GS-11		1.0			1.0
Private Lands Bio. GS-7/11			1.0		1.0
Private Lands Tech. GS-3/7			1.0		1.0
Law Enforment GS-11				1.0	1.0
Administration GS-9	1.0				1.0
Administration GS-7		1.0			1.0
Outdoor Rec. Planner		1.0			1.0
Maintenance WG-8	1.0			1.0	2.0
Maintenance WG-6			0.5		0.5
Tractor Operator WG-6			1.5	2.0	3.5
Totals	5.0	3.0	5.5	5.5	19.0

Step-down Management Plans

The CCP is intended as a broad umbrella Plan that provides general concepts; wildlife and habitat objectives; and endangered species, public use, and partnership objectives. Depending on Refuge needs, these may be very detailed or quite broad. The purpose of step-down management plans is to provide greater detail to managers to implement specific actions authorized by the CCP. The following table outlines the current and potential step-down management plans that apply to the Complex.

Step-down Management Plan	Status of Station Plan	Proprosed Revision Date
Safety Program / Operations	1998 Safety Plan	No revision necessary
Hazardous Material Oper.	1988 Hazardous Material Oper.	2005
Pollution Prevention	1997 Spill Prevention Plan	No revision necessary
Integrated Pest Management	2002 Integrated Pesticide Management Plan	2005
Refuge Uses (Compatibility)	1990 Compatibility Review	2002CCP
Visitor Services Plan	None	2003
Hunting	1983 Hunting Plan	2005
Fishing	None	2002
Cultural Resources	None	2006
Refuge Habitat Management Plan (HMP)	1973 Land Use Plan	2007
WMD Habitat Management Plan (HMP)		2012
Fire Management	1999 Fire Management Plan	No revision necessary
Wildlife Inventory Plan	1972	2012
Disease Prevention & Control	None	2004
Fisheries Resources Management	None	2002

Partnership Opportunities

Since the advent of the Partners for Fish and Wildlife Program in 1988, the Service's collective eyes have been opened to the potential for improvement of wildlife habitat on private land. Over 97 percent of the landscape of Waubay Wetland Management District is privately owned; to ignore private lands is folly with the hope of accomplishing landscape ecosystem management. In the past 12 years, funds and services have been contributed toward the wildlife improvement effort by the following individuals/ organizations: hundreds of landowners; Sisseton-Wahpeton Sioux Tribe; Federal Emergency Management Agency; Natural Resource Conservation Agency; Farm Service Agency; Grant, Day, Marshall, Roberts, Clark, and Codington County Soil and Water Conservation Districts; Friends of Big Stone Lake; Ducks Unlimited Inc.; South Dakota Game, Fish and Parks; Minnesota Area III Conservation Districts; Lake Farley Watershed; South Dakota Conservation Commission; North American Wetlands Conservation Council; Aberdeen Development Corporation; East Dakota Water Development District; Pheasants Forever; Big Stone Lake Watershed; Lake Kampeska Watershed; Lake Traverse Watershed; and others. Our private lands partners have chipped in to restore wetlands, create wetlands, restore grasslands, improve grasslands for wildlife, and other projects.

The limited environmental education program at Waubay NWR/WMD Complex has been aided by our partners at Glacial Lakes Outdoor School and the students and teachers of area schools. Many area school children have had the opportunity to enjoy their National Wildlife Refuge through the efforts of these dedicated individuals. The potential has barely been scratched, but the enthusiasm of the young people has let us know that we're providing a much-needed service.

These success stories give hope to fulfilling other needs. Potential partners for habitat conservation, wildlife observation, wildlife photography, environmental education and interpretation and other wildlife related recreation is limited only by one's imagination. Potential partners for these projects include conservation organizations, civic groups, tourism groups, State and Federal government agencies, individuals, corporations, and others.

Monitoring and Evaluation

The CCP identifies and incorporates monitoring and evaluation activities as strategies under the objectives developed for Waubay NWR and WMD. Each Complex program has specific guidelines described in the appropriate step-down plan. Step-down plans include approaches and methods to monitoring management activities and specific criteria to evaluate the outcomes of the activities. As new information becomes available through baseline data, research, or outcomes of management projects, the existing Complex programs would be adjusted. Step-down plans including the monitoring and evaluation sections would require periodic review, program evaluation, and adjustments, as necessary.

The Complex CCP will be a useful working document for present and future managers. Periodic review, evaluation, and the addition of information will be required to achieve effective implementation of the CCP, even as Refuge programs evolve over time.

Plan Amendment and Revision

The Waubay Project Leader will refer to the CCP annually to ensure station priorities and work guidance is on track with the CCP. Appropriate staff members will be assigned tasks and projects identified in the CCP to accomplish the objectives stated in the Plan. The Project Leader will review the CCP at least every 5 years to determine if it needs revision. Any necessary revisions will be incorporated into the Plan, with proper public participation. The Plan will be revised no later than 2017.

Environmental Action Statement

U.S. Fish & Wildlife Service
Region 6
Denver, Colorado

Within the spirit and intent of the Council on Environmental Quality's regulations for implementing the National Environmental Policy Act (NEPA) and other statutes, orders, and policies that protect fish and wildlife resources, I have established the following administrative record and have determined that the action of implementing the Waubay National Wildlife Refuge Complex Comprehensive Conservation Plan (CCP) is found not to have significant environmental effects as determined by the attached Finding of No Significant Impact and the Environmental Assessment as found in the Draft CCP.

Ralph O. Morgenweck, Regional Director   8/34/02
Region 6, U.S. Fish & Wildlife Service   Date

Richard A. Coleman, PhD   8/30/02
Regional Chief, National Wildlife Refuge System   Date
Refuges and Wildlife

Ron Shupe, Refuge Program Supervisor   8/19/02
National Wildlife Refuge System   Date
Refuges and Wildlife

Larry D. Martin, Project Leader   23 Aug 2002
Waubay NWR Complex   Date

Finding of No Significant Impact

Waubay National Wildlife Refuge Complex
Comprehensive Conservation Plan

Three management alternatives for the Waubay National Wildlife Refuge Complex were assessed as to their effectiveness in achieving the Refuge purposes and their impact on the human environment. Alternative A, the No Action Alternative, would continue current management of the Refuge and Wetland Management District (WMD). Alternative B, the Tallgrass Prairie Alternative, would focus on protecting and restoring tallgrass prairie in the Minnesota-Red River Lowlands of the WMD. Alternative C, Enhanced Management, the preferred alternative, would increase management of Complex habitats and public use opportunities. Based on this assessment and comments received, I have selected the preferred Alternative C for implementation.

The preferred alternative was selected because it best meets the purpose of the Complex as a refuge and breeding ground for migratory birds and other wildlife. The preferred alternative will also provide public access for wildlife-dependent recreation, environmental education, and interpretation.

I find that the preferred alternative is not a major Federal action that would significantly affect the quality of the human environment within the meaning of Section 102(2)(C) of the National Environmental Policy Act of 1969. Accordingly, the preparation of an Environmental Impact Statement on the proposed action is not required.

The following is a summary of anticipated environmental effects from implementation of the preferred alternative:

- The preferred alternative will not adversely impact endangered or threatened species or their habitat.
- The preferred alternative will not adversely impact archaeological or historical resources.
- The preferred alternative will not adversely impact wetlands nor does the plan call for structures that could be damaged by or that would significantly influence the movement of floodwater.
- The preferred alternative will not have a disproportionately high or adverse human health or environmental effect on minority or low-income populations.
- The State of South Dakota has been notified and given the opportunity to review the Comprehensive Conservation Plan and associated Environmental Assessment.

ACTING _____

Regional Director, Region 6
U.S. Fish and Wildlife Service
Denver, Colorado

_____8/30/02_____
Date

Appendix A. Wildlife Species of Waubay Complex

BIRDS

This list is based on the reference <u>The Birds of South Dakota</u> (South Dakota Ornithologists' Union 1991) along with staff observations.

Loons
* Common Loon   *Gavia immer*

Grebes
Pied-billed Grebe   *Podilymbus podiceps*
Horned Grebe   *Podiceps auritus*
Red-necked Grebe   *Podiceps grisegena*
Eared Grebe   *Podiceps nigricollis*
Western Grebe   *Aechmophorus occidentalis*
Clark's Grebe   *Aechmophorus clarkii*

Pelicans
American White Pelican   *Pelecanus erythrorhynchos*

Cormorants
Double-crested Cormorant   *Phalacrocorax auritus*

Bitterns, Herons, and Egrets
* American Bittern   *Botaurus lentiginosus*
Least Bittern   *Ixobrychus exilis*
Great Blue Heron   *Ardea herodias*
Great Egret   *Ardea alba*
Snowy Egret   *Egretta thula*
Little Blue Heron   *Egretta caerulea*
Cattle Egret   *Bubulcus ibis*
Green Heron   *Butorides virescens*
Black-crowned Night-Heron   *Nycticorax nycticorax*

Ibises and Spoonbills
* White-faced Ibis   *Plegadis chihi*

New World Vultures
Turkey Vulture   *Cathartes aura*

Swans, Geese, and Ducks
Greater White-fronted Goose   *Anser albifrons*
Snow Goose   *Chen caerulescens*
Ross' Goose   *Chen rossii*
Canada Goose   *Branta canadensis*
Tundra Swan   *Cygnus columbianus*
Wood Duck   *Aix sponsa*
Gadwall   *Anas strepera*
American Wigeon   *Anas americana*
American Black Duck   *Anas rubripes*
Mallard   *Anas platyrhynchos*
Blue-winged Teal   *Anas discors*
Cinnamon Teal   *Anas cyanoptera*
Northern Shoveler   *Anas clypeata*
Northern Pintail   *Anas acuta*
Green-winged Teal   *Anas crecca*
Canvasback   *Aythya valisineria*
Redhead   *Aythya americana*
Ring-necked Duck   *Aythya collaris*
Lesser Scaup   *Aythya affinis*
Surf Scoter   *Melanitta perspicillata*
White-winged Scoter   *Melanitta fusca*
Long-tailed Duck   *Clangula hyemalis*
Bufflehead   *Bucephala albeola*
Common Goldeneye   *Bucephala clangula*
Hooded Merganser   *Lophodytes cucullatus*
Common Merganser   *Mergus merganser*

Red-breasted Merganser   *Mergus serrator*
Ruddy Duck   *Oxyura jamaicensis*

Osprey, Kites, Hawks, and Eagles
Osprey   *Pandion haliaetus*
Bald Eagle   *Haliaeetus leucocephalus*
* Northern Harrier   *Circus cyaneus*
Sharp-shinned Hawk   *Accipiter striatus*
Cooper's Hawk   *Accipiter cooperii*
* Northern Goshawk   *Accipiter gentilis*
Broad-winged Hawk   *Buteo platypterus*
Swainson's Hawk   *Buteo swainsoni*
Red-tailed Hawk   *Buteo jamaicensis*
* Ferruginous Hawk   *Buteo regalis*
Rough-legged Hawk   *Buteo lagopus*
Golden Eagle   *Aquila chrysaetos*

Falcons and Caracaras
American Kestrel   *Falco sparverius*
Merlin   *Falco columbarius*
* Peregrine Falcon   *Falco peregrinus*
Prairie Falcon   *Falco mexicanus*

Gallinaceous Birds
Gray Partridge   Introduced   *Perdix perdix*
Ring-necked Pheasant Introduced *Phasianus colchicus*
Sharp-tailed Grouse   *Tympanuchus phasianellus*
Greater Prairie-Chicken   *Tympanuchus cupido*

Rails
Virginia Rail   *Rallus limicola*
Sora   *Porzana carolina*
Common Moorhen   *Gallinula chloropus*
American Coot   *Fulica americana*

Cranes
Sandhill Crane   *Grus canadensis*
Whooping Crane   *Grus americana*

Plovers
Black-bellied Plover   *Pluvialis squatarola*
American Golden-Plover   *Pluvialis dominica*
Semipalmated Plover   *Charadrius semipalmatus*
Piping Plover   *Charadrius melodus*
Killdeer   *Charadrius vociferus*

Stilts and Avocets
American Avocet   *Recurvirostra americana*

Sandpipers and Phalaropes
Greater Yellowlegs   *Tringa melanoleuca*
Lesser Yellowlegs   *Tringa flavipes*
Solitary Sandpiper   *Tringa solitaria*
Willet   *Catoptrophorus semipalmatus*
Spotted Sandpiper   *Actitis macularia*
* Upland Sandpiper   *Bartramia longicauda*
* Long-billed Curlew   *Numenius americanus*
Hudsonian Godwit   *Limosa haemastica*
Marbled Godwit   *Limosa fedoa*
Ruddy Turnstone   *Arenaria interpres*
Sanderling   *Calidris alba*
Semipalmated Sandpiper   *Calidris pusilla*
Least Sandpiper   *Calidris minutilla*
White-rumped Sandpiper   *Calidris fuscicollis*
Baird's Sandpiper   *Calidris bairdii*
Pectoral Sandpiper   *Calidris melanotos*
Dunlin   *Calidris alpina*
Stilt Sandpiper   *Calidris himantopus*
Buff-breasted Sandpiper   *Tryngites subruficollis*
Short-billed Dowitcher   *Limnodromus griseus*
Long-billed Dowitcher   *Limnodromus scolopaceus*
Common Snipe   *Gallinago gallinago*

American Woodcock	*Scolopax minor*	**Vireos**	
Wilson's Phalarope	*Phalaropus tricolor*	Yellow-throated Vireo	*Vireo flavifrons*
Red-necked Phalarope	*Phalaropus lobatus*	Warbling Vireo	*Vireo gilvus*
		Philadelphia Vireo	*Vireo philadelphicus*
Skuas, Jaegers, Gulls, and Terns		Red-eyed Vireo	*Vireo olivaceus*
Franklin's Gull	*Larus pipixcan*		
Bonaparte's Gull	*Larus philadelphia*	**Crows, Jays, and Magpies**	
Ring-billed Gull	*Larus delawarensis*	Blue Jay	*Cyanocitta cristata*
California Gull	*Larus californicus*	Black-billed Magpie	*Pica hudsonia*
Herring Gull	*Larus argentatus*	American Crow	*Corvus brachyrhynchos*
Common Tern	*Sterna hirundo*		
Forster's Tern	*Sterna forsteri*	**Larks**	
* Black Tern	*Chlidonias niger*	Horned Lark	*Eremophila alpestris*
Pigeons and Doves		**Swallows**	
Mourning Dove	*Zenaida macroura*	Purple Martin	*Progne subis*
Passenger Pigeon EXTINCT	*Ectopistes migratorius*	Tree Swallow	*Tachycineta bicolor*
		Northern Rough-winged Swallow	
Cuckoos and Anis			*Stelgidopteryx serripennis*
Black-billed Cuckoo	*Coccyzus erythropthalmus*	Bank Swallow	*Riparia riparia*
Yellow-billed Cuckoo	*Coccyzus americanus*	Cliff Swallow	*Petrochelidon pyrrhonota*
		Barn Swallow	*Hirundo rustica*
Typical Owls			
Eastern Screech-Owl	*Otus asio*	**Titmice and Chickadees**	
Great Horned Owl	*Bubo virginianus*	Black-capped Chickadee	*Poecile atricapilla*
Snowy Owl	*Nyctea scandiaca*		
* Burrowing Owl	*Athene cunicularia*	**Nuthatches**	
Long-eared Owl	*Asio otus*	Red-breasted Nuthatch	*Sitta canadensis*
Short-eared Owl	*Asio flammeus*	White-breasted Nuthatch	*Sitta carolinensis*
Boreal Owl	*Aegolius funereus*		
Northern Saw-whet Owl	*Aegolius acadicus*	**Creepers**	
		Brown Creeper	*Certhia americana*
Nightjars			
Common Nighthawk	*Chordeiles minor*	**Wrens**	
Whip-poor-will	*Caprimulgus vociferus*	House Wren	*Troglodytes aedon*
		* Sedge Wren	*Cistothorus platensis*
Swifts		Marsh Wren	*Cistothorus palustris*
Chimney Swift	*Chaetura pelagica*		
		Kinglets	
Hummingbirds		Golden-crowned Kinglet	*Regulus satrapa*
Ruby-throated Hummingbird	*Archilochus colubris*	Ruby-crowned Kinglet	*Regulus calendula*
Kingfishers		**Thrushes**	
Belted Kingfisher	*Ceryle alcyon*	Eastern Bluebird	*Sialia sialis*
		* Veery	*Catharus fuscescens*
Woodpeckers		Gray-cheeked Thrush	*Catharus minimus*
* Red-headed Woodpecker	*Melanerpes erythrocephalus*	Swainson's Thrush	*Catharus ustulatus*
Red-bellied Woodpecker	*Melanerpes carolinus*	Hermit Thrush	*Catharus guttatus*
Yellow-bellied Sapsucker	*Sphyrapicus varius*	American Robin	*Turdus migratorius*
Downy Woodpecker	*Picoides pubescens*		
Hairy Woodpecker	*Picoides villosus*	**Mimic Thrushes**	
Northern Flicker	*Colaptes auratus*	Gray Catbird	*Dumetella carolinensis*
Pileated Woodpecker	*Dryocopus pileatus*	Northern Mockingbird	*Mimus polyglottos*
		Brown Thrasher	*Toxostoma rufum*
Tyrant Flycatchers			
* Olive-sided Flycatcher	*Contopus cooperi*	**Starlings**	
Eastern Wood-Pewee	*Contopus virens*	European Starling	*Sturnus vulgaris*
Yellow-bellied Flycatcher	*Empidonax flaviventris*		
Alder Flycatcher	*Empidonax alnorum*	**Wagtails and Pipits**	
Willow Flycatcher	*Empidonax traillii*	American (Water) Pipit	*Anthus rubescens*
Least Flycatcher	*Empidonax minimus*		
Eastern Phoebe	*Sayornis phoebe*	**Waxwings**	
Great Crested Flycatcher	*Myiarchus crinitus*	Bohemian Waxwing	*Bombycilla garrulus*
Western Kingbird	*Tyrannus verticalis*	Cedar Waxwing	*Bombycilla cedrorum*
Eastern Kingbird	*Tyrannus tyrannus*		
Scissor-tailed Flycatcher	*Tyrannus forficatus*	**Wood Warblers**	
		Tennessee Warbler	*Vermivora peregrina*
Shrikes		Orange-crowned Warbler	*Vermivora celata*
* Loggerhead Shrike	*Lanius ludovicianus*	Nashville Warbler	*Vermivora ruficapilla*
Northern Shrike	*Lanius excubitor*	Northern Parula	*Parula americana*
		Yellow Warbler	*Dendroica petechia*
		Chestnut-sided Warbler	*Dendroica pensylvanica*

Magnolia Warbler	*Dendroica magnolia*	Pine Siskin	*Carduelis pinus*
Cape May Warbler	*Dendroica tigrina*	American Goldfinch	*Carduelis tristis*
Yellow-rumped Warbler	*Dendroica coronata*	Evening Grosbeak	*Coccothraustes vespertinus*

Magnolia Warbler		*Dendroica magnolia*
Cape May Warbler		*Dendroica tigrina*
Yellow-rumped Warbler		*Dendroica coronata*
Blackburnian Warbler		*Dendroica fusca*
Palm Warbler		*Dendroica palmarum*
Bay-breasted Warbler		*Dendroica castanea*
Blackpoll Warbler		*Dendroica striata*
Black-and-white Warbler		*Mniotilta varia*
American Redstart		*Setophaga ruticilla*
Ovenbird		*Seiurus aurocapillus*
Northern Waterthrush		*Seiurus noveboracensis*
Mourning Warbler		*Oporornis philadelphia*
Common Yellowthroat		*Geothlypis trichas*
Wilson's Warbler		*Wilsonia pusilla*
Canada Warbler		*Wilsonia canadensis*
Yellow-breasted Chat		*Icteria virens*

Tanagers
Scarlet Tanager	*Piranga olivacea*

Sparrows and Towhees
Spotted Towhee	*Pipilo maculatus*
American Tree Sparrow	*Spizella arborea*
Chipping Sparrow	*Spizella passerina*
Clay-colored Sparrow	*Spizella pallida*
Field Sparrow	*Spizella pusilla*
Vesper Sparrow	*Pooecetes gramineus*
Lark Sparrow	*Chondestes grammacus*
* Lark Bunting	*Calamospiza melanocorys*
Savannah Sparrow	*Passerculus sandwichensis*
* Grasshopper Sparrow	*Ammodramus savannarum*
Le Conte's Sparrow	*Ammodramus leconteii*
Nelson's Sharp-tailed Sparrow	*Ammodramus nelsoni*
Fox Sparrow	*Passerelia iliaca*
Song Sparrow	*Melospiza melodia*
Lincoln's Sparrow	*Melospiza lincolnii*
Swamp Sparrow	*Melospiza georgiana*
White-throated Sparrow	*Zonotrichia albicollis*
Harris' Sparrow	*Zonotrichia querula*
White-crowned Sparrow	*Zonotrichia leucophrys*
Dark-eyed Junco	*Junco hyemalis*
Lapland Longspur	*Calcarius lapponicus*
* Chestnut-collared Longspur	*Calcarius ornatus*
Snow Bunting	*Plectrophenax nivalis*

Cardinals, Grosbeaks, and Allies
Rose-breasted Grosbeak	*Pheucticus ludovicianus*
Lazuli Bunting	*Passerina amoena*
Indigo Bunting	*Passerina cyanea*
* Dickcissel	*Spiza americana*

Blackbirds and Orioles
Bobolink	*Dolichonyx oryzivorus*
Red-winged Blackbird	*Agelaius phoeniceus*
Western Meadowlark	*Surnella neglecta*
Yellow-headed Blackbird	
	Xanthocephalus xanthocephalus
Rusty Blackbird	*Euphagus carolinus*
Brewer's Blackbird	*Euphagus cyanocephalus*
Common Grackle	*Quiscalus quiscula*
Brown-headed Cowbird	*Molothrus ater*
Orchard Oriole	*Icterus spurius*
Baltimore Oriole	*Icterus galbula*

Finches
Pine Grosbeak	*Pinicola enucleator*
Purple Finch	*Carpodacus purpureus*
House Finch	*Carpodacus mexicanus*
Red Crossbill	*Loxia curvirostra*
White-winged Crossbill	*Loxia leucoptera*
Common Redpoll	*Carduelis flammea*
Hoary Redpoll	*Carduelis hornemanni*

Old World Sparrows
House Sparrow Introduced	*Passer domesticus*

*Migratory Nongame Birds of Management Concern in the United States: The 1995 List

MAMMALS

This list is based on the reference <u>Wild Mammals of South Dakota</u> (Higgins et al. 2000) along with staff observations.

Opossums
Virginia Opossum	*Didelphis virginiana*

Insectivores
Shrews
Cinereus or Masked Shrew	*Sorex cinereus*
Northern Short-tailed Shrew	*Blarina brevicauda*
Arctic Shrew	*Sorex arcticus*
Hayden's Shrew	*Sorex haydeni*
Water Shrew	*Sorex palustris*
Pygmy Shrew	*Sorex hoyi*

Bats
Vespertilionid Bats
Little Brown Myotis	*Myotis lucifugus*
Northern Myotis	*Myotis septentrionalis*
Eastern Red Bat	*Lasiurus borealis*
Hoary Bat	*Lasiurus cinereus*
Silver-haired Bat	*Lasionycteris noctivagans*
Big Brown Bat	*Eptesicus fuscus*

Lagomorphs
Hares and Rabbits
Eastern Cottontail	*Sylvilagus floridanus*
White-tailed Jackrabbit	*Lepus townsendii*

Rodents
Squirrels
Eastern Chipmunk	*Tamias striatus*
Woodchuck	*Marmota monax*
Franklin's Ground Squirrel	*Spermophilus franklinii*
Richardson's Ground Squirrel	
	Spermophilus richardsonii
Thirteen-lined Ground Squirrel	
	Spermophilus tridecemlineatus
Eastern Gray Squirrel	*Sciurus carolinensis*
Eastern Fox Squirrel	*Sciurus niger*

Pocket Gophers
Northern Pocket Gopher	*Thomomys talpoides*
Plains Pocket Gopher	*Geomys bursarius*

Heteromyids
Plains Pocket Mouse	*Perognathus flavescens*

Beavers
American Beaver	*Castor canadensis*

Mice, Rats, and Voles
Western Harvest Mouse	*Reithrodontomys megalotis*
White-footed Mouse	*Peromyscus leucopus*
Deer Mouse	*Peromyscus maniculatus*
Northern Grasshopper Mouse	*Onychomys leucogaster*
Norway Rat	*Rattus norvegicus*
House Mouse	*Mus musculus*
Southern Red-backed Vole	*Clethrionomys gapperi*
Prairie Vole	*Microtus ochrogaster*
Meadow Vole	*Microtus pennsylvanicus*
Common Muskrat	*Ondatra zibethicus*

Jumping Mice
  Meadow Jumping Mouse .... *Zapus hudsonius*
  Western Jumping Mouse .... *Zapus princeps*
New World Porcupines
  Common Porcupine .... *Erethizon dorsatum*

Carnivores
Canids
  Coyote .... *Canis latrans*
  Red Fox .... *Vulpes vulpes*
  Common Gray Fox .... *Urocyon cinereoargenteus*
Procyonids
  Common Raccoon .... *Procyon lotor*
Mustelids
  Ermine .... *Mustela erminea*
  Long-tailed Weasel .... *Mustela frenata*
  Least Weasel .... *Mustela nivalis*
  American Mink .... *Mustela vison*
  American Badger .... *Taxidea taxus*
  Northern River Otter .... *Lutra canadensis*
Mephitids
  Eastern Spotted Skunk .... *Spilogale putorius*
  Striped Skunk .... *Mephitis mephitis*
Cats
  Feral Cat .... *Felis catus*
  Bobcat .... *Felis rufus*
Cervids
  Wapiti or Elk .... *Cervus elaphus*
  Mule or Black-tailed Deer .... *Odocoileus hemionus*
  White-tailed Deer .... *Odocoileus virginianus*
  Moose .... *Alces alces*
Pronghorn
  Pronghorn .... *Antilocapra americana*
Bovids
  American Bison .... *Bos bison*
  Domestic cattle .... *Bos taurus*

AMPHIBIANS AND REPTILES

This list is based on the reference <u>A Field Guide to South Dakota Amphibians</u> (Fischer et al. 1999) and <u>A Field Guide to Reptiles and Amphibians</u> (Conant and Collins 1991), along with staff observations.

Salamanders
  Tiger Salamander .... *Ambistoma tigrinum*
  Mudpuppy .... *Necturus maculosus*

Frogs and Toads
  Chorus Frog .... *Pseudacris triseriata*
  Northern Leopard Frog .... *Rana pipiens*
  Wood Frog .... *Rana sylvatica*
  Eastern Grey Treefrog .... *Hyla versicolor*
  Woodhouse's Toad .... *Bufo woodhousei*
  American Toad .... *Bufo americanus*
  Canadian Toad .... *Bufo hemiophrys*
  Great Plains Toad .... *Bufo cognatus*

Turtles
  Western Painted Turtle .... *Chrysemys picta bellii*
  Snapping Turtle .... *Chelydra serpentina*
  Spiny Soft Shelled Turtle .... *Trionyx spiniferus*

Snakes
  Eastern Garter Snake .... *Thamnophis sirtalis sirtalis*
  Plains Garter Snake .... *Thamnophis radix*
  Smooth Green Snake .... *Opheodrys vernalis*
  Northern Redbelly Snake .... *Storeria occipitomaculata*
  Western Hognose Snake .... *Heterodon nasicus*
  Bullsnake .... *Pituophis melanoleucus*
  Northern Prairie skink .... *Eumeces septentrionalis*

FISH

This list is based on the reference <u>Guide to the Common Fishes of South Dakota</u> (Neumann and Willis 1994) along with staff observations.

American Eel .... *Anguilla rostrata*
Black Bullhead .... *Ameiurus melas*
Yellow Bullhead .... *Ameiurus natalis*
Stonecat .... *Noturus flavus*
Channel Catfish .... *Ictalurus punctatus*
Common Carp .... *Cyprinus carpio*
White Sucker .... *Catostomus commersoni*
Bigmouth Buffalo .... *Ictiobus cyprinellus*
River Carpsucker .... *Carpiodes carpio*
Shorthead Redhorse .... *Moxostoma macrolepidotum*
Freshwater Drum .... *Aplodinotus grunniens*
Central Mudminnow .... *Umbra limi*
Banded Killifish .... *Fundulus diaphanus*
Fathead Minnow .... *Pimephales promelas*
Emerald Shiner .... *Notropis atherinoides*
Common Shiner .... *Luxilus cornutus*
Golden Shiner .... *Notemigonus crysoleucas*
Creek Chub .... *Semotilus atromaculatus*
Northern Redbelly Dace .... *Phoxinus eos*
Brook Stickleback .... *Culaea inconstans*
Trout-perch .... *Percopsis omiscomaycus*
Topeka Shiner .... *Notropis topeka*
Logperch .... *Percina caprodes*
Johnny Darter .... *Etheostoma nigrum*
White Bass .... *Morone chrysops*
Rock Bass .... *Ambloplites rupestris*
Smallmouth Bass .... *Micropterus dolomieu*
Largemouth Bass .... *Micropterus salmoides*
Bluegill .... *Lepornis macrochirus*
Pumpkinseed .... *Lepomis gibbosus*
Green Sunfish .... *Lepomis cyanellus*
Orange-spotted Sunfish .... *Lepomis humilis*
Black Crappie .... *Pomoxis nigromaculatus*
White Crappie .... *Pomoxis annularis*
Yellow Perch .... *Perca flavescens*
Walleye .... *Stizostedion vitreum*
Saugeye .... *Stizostedion spp.*
Northern Pike .... *Esox lucius*
Muskellunge .... *Esox masquinongy*

Appendix B. References

Amaral, M., A. Kozol, and T. French. 1997. Conservation status and reintroduction of the endangered American burying beetle. Northeastern Naturalist 4(3):121-132.

Anderson, R.S. 1982. On the decreasing abundance of *Nicrophorus americanus* Olivier (Coleoptera: Silphidae) in eastern North America. Coleopterists Bulletin, 36:362-365.

Anderson, M., P. Bourgeron, M.T. Bryer, R. Crawford, L. Engelking, D. Faber-Langendoen, M. Gallyoun, K. Goodin, D.H. Grossman, S. Landaal, K. Metzler, K.D. Patterson, M. Pyne, M. Reid, L. Sneddon, and A.S. Weakley. 1998. International classification of ecological communities: terrestrial vegetation of the United States. Volume II. The National Vegetation Classification System: list of types. The Nature Conservancy, Arlington, VA.

Apfelbaum, S. I., and K.A. Chapman. 1996. Ecological restoration: A practical approach *In* : M.S. Boyce and A. W. Haney (eds .) Ecosystem Management: Applications for Sustainable Forest and Wildlife Resources. Yale University Press, New Haven, CT.

Backlund, D., and G. Marrone. 1995. Surveys for the endangered American burying beetle (Nicrophorus americanus) in Gregory, Tripp and Todd counties, South Dakota, August, 1995. South Dakota Game, Fish and Parks report.

Baldassarre, G.A., and E.G. Bolen. 1994. Waterfowl Ecology and Management. John Wiley and Sons, Inc., NY. 609pp.

Barker, W.T., K.K. Sedivec, T.A. Messmer, K.F. Higgins, and D.R. Hertel. 1990. Effects of specialized grazing systems on waterfowl production in southcentral North Dakota. *Trans. North Am. Wildl. Nat. Resourc. Conf. 55:462-474.*

Barngrover, L. 1974. W.E. Kirch Wildlife Management Area resource inventory and long range plan summary. Nevada Department of Fish and Game. 12pp.

Batt, B.D.J., M.G. Anderson, C. D. Anderson, and F. D. Caswill. 1989. The Use of Prairie Potholes by North American Ducks. Pages 204-227 in A. Vandervalk, ed. Northern Prairie Wetlands. Iowa State Univ. Press, Ames. IA.

Beard, E.R. 1953. The importance of beaver in waterfowl management at the Seney National Wildlife Refuge. *Journal of Wildlife Management* 17:398-436.

Bell, D.V., and L.W. Austin. 1985. The game fishing season and its effects on overwintering wildfowl. *Biological Conservation* 17: 183-206

Berkey, G., D. Johnson, R. Crawford, D. Lambeth, S. Galipeau, and R. Kreil. 1993. A review of wildlife management practices in North Dakota: Effects on nongame bird populations and habitats. Unpublished report submitted to U.S. Fish & Wildlife Service, Region 6, Denver, CO. 51pp.

Bouffard, S.H. 1982. Wildlife values versus human recreation: Ruby Lake National Wildlife Refuge. Transactions of the North American Wildlife and Natural Resources Conference 47:553-558.

Bradley, L.E.,and W. Ranney. 1985. Archaeological survey and testing of a proposed construction site at Waubay Wildlife Refuge, Waubay, South Dakota. Dakota Interactive Services Inc., Vermillion, South Dakota. prepared for the U.S. Fish & Wildlife Service.

Braun, C.E., K.W. Harmon, J.A. Jackson, and C.D. Littlefield. 1978. Management of National Wildlife Refuges in the United States: its impacts on birds. *Wilson Bulletin* 90:309-321.

Brittingham, M.C., and S.A. Temple. 1983. Have Cowbirds caused forest songbirds to decline? *Bioscience* 33: 31-35.

Burger, L.D., L.W. Burger Jr., and J. Faaborg. 1994. Effects of prairie fragmentation on predation on artificial nests. *Journal of Wildlife Management* 58:249-254.

Coggins, et al 1987

Conant, R., and J.T. Collins. 1991. Field Guide to Reptiles and Amphibians- Eastern and Central North America. Houghton Mifflin Company, Boston. 450 pp.

Cooke, A.S. 1987. Disturbance by anglers of birds at Grafham Water. ITE Symposium 19:15-22.

Cowardin, L.M., V. Carter, F.C. Golet, and E.T. LaRoe. 1979. Classification of Wetlands and Deepwater Habitats of the United States. U.S. Department of the Interior, Fish & Wildlife Service, FWS/OBS-79/31. Washington, D.C. 131 pp.

Dahl, T.E. 1990. Wetlands losses in the United States 1780s to 1980s. U.S. Department of the Interior, Fish & Wildlife Service, Washington, DC. 13 pp.

Dobkin, D.S. 1992. Neotropical Migrant Land birds in the Northern Rockies and Great Plains. USDA Forest Service Northern Region. Publication No. R1-93-34. Missoula, MT.

Duebbert, H.F., E.T. Jacobson, K.F. Higgins and E.B. Podoll. 1981. Establishment of seeded grasslands for wildlife habitat in the Prairie Pothole Region. U.S. Fish & Wildlife Service. Spec. Sci. Rep.- Wildl. 234. 21 pp.

Duebbert, H.F., and H.A. Kantrud. 1974. Upland duck nesting related to land use and predator reduction. *J. Wildl. Manage.* 38:257-265.

Edwards, R., and D. Bell. 1985. Fishing in troubled waters. New Science 1446, 7 March: 19-21.

Ehrlich, P.R., D.S. Dobkin, and D. Wheye. 1988. The Birder's Handbook: A Field Guide to the Natural History of North American Birds. Simon and Schuster, Inc., New York, 785 pp.

Evenson, D.E. 1974. Migratory waterfowl use of Houghton Lake, Michigan. M.S. thesis, University of Michigan, Ann Arbor. 105 pp.

Faanes, C.A. 1987. Breeding birds and vegetation structure in western North Dakota wooded draws. *Prairie Nat.* 19: 209-220

Fischer, T.D., D.C. Backlund, K.F. Higgins, and D.E. Naugle. 1999. Field guide to South Dakota amphibians. SDAES Bulletin 733. South Dakota State Univ., Brookings. 52 pp.

Frayer, W.E., T.J. Monahan, D.C. Bowden and F.A. Graybill. 1983. Status and trends of wetlands and deepwater habitats in the conterminous United States, 1950s to 1970s. Dep. Forest and Wood Sciences, Colorado State Univ. Ft. Collins, CO. 31 pp.

Gates, J.E., and L.W. Gysel. 1978. Avian nest dispersion and fledging success in field-forest ecotones. *Ecology* 59: 871-883.

Heitmeyer, M.E. 1985. Wintering strategies of female mallards related to dynamics of lowland hardwood wetlands in the upper Mississippi Delta. PH.D. thesis, University of Missouri, Colombia. 376pp.

Herkert, J.R. 1994. The effects of habitat fragmentation on Midwestern grassland bird communities. *Ecological Applications* 4:461-471.

Hertel, D. R. 1987. Effects of grazing systems on habitats used by upland nesting waterfowl in south central North Dakota. North Dakota State University of Agriculture and Applied Science. 94pp.

Higgins, K.F., E.D. Stukel, J.M. Goulet, and D. C. Backlund. 2000. Wild Mammals of South Dakota. SD Game, Fish and Parks. 278 pp.

Higgins, K.F., V.J. Smith, J.A. Jenks, J.J. Higgins, and G.A. Wolbrink. 2001. A provisional inventory of relic tallgrass tracts remaining in eastern South Dakota. South Dakota Coop. Fish and Wildl. Res. Unit.

Hodorff, R.A., C.H. Sieg, and R.L. Linder. 1988. Wildlife Response to stand structure of deciduous woodlands. *Journal of Wildlife Management.* 52:667-673.

Hopkins, R.B., J.F. Cassel, and A.J. Bjugstad. 1986. Relationships between breeding birds and vegetation in four woodland types of the Little Missouri National Grasslands. USDA For. Serv. Res. Pap. RM-270.

Jackson, M.A. and D.L. Toom. 1999. Cultural Resources Overview Studies of the Tewaukon National Wildlife Refuge, Sargent County, North Dakota and the Waubay National Wildlife Refuge, Day County, South Dakota. Department of Anthropology, Univ. of No. Dakota, Grand Forks.

Jahn, L.R., and R.A. Hunt. 1964. Duck and Coot ecology and management in Wisconsin. Wisconsin Conservation Dept. Technical Bulletin 33, Madison, WI. 164 pp.

Johnson, J.R., and G.E. Larson. 1999. Grassland Plants of South Dakota and the Northern Great Plains. SDSU, College of Agriculture and Biological Sciences. Brookings, SD. 288 pp.

Johnson, R.E. 1964. Fish and fowl. Pages 453-458 in J.P. Linduska, ed. Waterfowl tomorrow. U.S. Department of Interior, U.S. Fish & Wildlife Service. U.S. Government Printing Office, Washington, D.C.

Johnson, R.G., and S.A. Temple. 1990. Nest predation and brood parasitism of tallgrass prairie birds. *Journal of Wildlife Management.* 54:106-111.

Johnson, R.R., and K.F. Higgins. 1997. Wetland Resources of Eastern South Dakota. South Dakota State University. Brookings, SD.102 pp.

Keith, L.B. 1961. A study of waterfowl ecology on small impoundments in southeastern Alberta Wildlife Monograph 6, The Wildlife Society, Washington, D.C. 88 pp.

Keller, S.W., and K.P. Zimmerman. 1981. Cultural Resource Investigations of the Waubay National Wildlife Refuge. Dakota Interactive Services, Inc., Vermillion, SD.

Kirsch, L.M., H.F. Duebbert, and A.D. Kruse.1978. Grazing and haying effects on habitats of upland nesting birds. *Trans. North America Wildl. and Nat. Resour. Conf.* 43:486-497.

Knickerbocker, B. 1869. Medical history of Fort Wadsworth, Vol. l, Book 392, National Archives.

Knopf, F.L. 1994. Avian assemblages on altered grasslands. *Studies in Avian Biology No.* 15:247-257.

Korschgen, C.E., L.S. George, and W.L. Green. 1985. Disturbance of diving ducks by boaters on a migrational staging area. *Wildlife Society Bulletin* 13:290-296.

Korschgen, C.E. and R.B. Dahlgren. 1992. Human Disturbances of Waterfowl: Causes, Effects, and Management. Fish and Wildlife Leaflet 13, Washington, D.C.

Kusler, J.A., and G. Brooks. (Eds.) 1987. Proceedings of the national wetland symposium: Wetland Hydrology. Association of State Wetland Managers. Berne, NY. 339 pp.

Leoschke, M. J. 1997. The prairie coteau natural areas inventory: Day, Marshall, and Roberts Counties, South Dakota. Midwest Regional Office. The Nature Conservancy Minneapolis, MN. 56 pp.

Liddle, M.J., and H.R.A. Scorgie. 1980. The effects of recreation on freshwater plants and animals: a review. *Biological Conservation* 33: 65-80.

Lomolino, M.V., and J.C. Creighton. 1996. Habitat selection, breeding success and conservation of the endangered American burying beetle (*Nicrophorus americanus*). *Biological Conservation* 77:235-241.

Madden, E.M. 1996. Passerine communities and bird-habitat relationships on prescribe-burned, mixed-grass prairie in North Dakota. M.S. Thesis. Montana State University, Bozeman. 153 pp.

Madsen, C. Personal communication. State Private Lands Coordinator, USFWS. Brookings, SD.

Mendall, H.L. 1958. The ring-necked duck in the northeast. University of Maine Bulletin, Vol. LX, No. 16. University of Maine Studies, Second Series, No. 73. 317 pp.

Minnesota Department of Natural Resources. 1991. Western Prairie Fringed Orchid.

Mitsch, W.J., and J.G. Gosselink. 1986. Wetlands. Van Nostrand Reinhold Co., New York. 539 pp

Moffat, M., and N. McPhillips. 1993. Management for butterflies in the Northern Great Plains: A literature review and guidebook for land managers. U.S. Fish & Wildlife Service. Washington D.C. 19 pp.

National Park Service. 1998. How to Apply National Register Criteria for Evaluation. National Register Bulletin 15. Cultural Resources Division, National Park Service, U.S. Department of the Interior, Washington, D.C.

The Nature Conservancy Northern Tallgrass Prairie Ecoregional Planning Team. 1998. Ecoregional planning in the northern tallgrass prairie ecoregion. The Nature Conservancy. Midwest Regional Office, Minneapolis, MN, 208 pp

Naugle, D.E., K.F. Higgins, and K.K. Bakker. 2000. A synthesis of the effects of upland management practices on waterfowl and other birds in the northern great plains of the U.S. and Canada. College of Natural Resources, University of Wisconsin- Stevens Point. Wildlife Technical Report 1. 28 pp.

Neumann, R.M., and D.W. Willis. 1994. Guide to the Common Fishes of South Dakota. Dept. of Wildlife and Fisheries Sciences- South Dakota State University, SD Game, Fish and Parks, and South Dakota Cooperative Extension Service. 60 pp.

Niehus, C.A., A.V. Vecchia, and R.F. Thompson. 1999. Lake-Level Frequency Analysis for the Waubay Lakes Chain, Northeastern South Dakota. Water-Resources Investigations Report 99-4122. U.S. Dept. of the Interior, U.S. Geological Survey. Rapid City, SD.

Niehus, C.A., A.V. Vecchia and R.F. Thompson. 1999a. Supplement to Water-Resources Investigation Report 99-4122, Lake-Level Frequency Analysis for the Waubay Lakes Chain, Northeastern South Dakota. Water-Resources Investigations Report 99-4251. U.S. Dept. of the Interior, U.S. Geological Survey. Rapid City, SD.

Noss, R.F., G.T. La Roe III, and J.M. Scott. 1995. Endangered Ecosystems of the United States: A Preliminary Assessment of Loss and Degradation. Biological Report 28, National Biological Service. Washington, D.C. 58 pp.

Okroi, D. Personal communication. Administrative Officer, USFWS. Waubay NWR.

Peterson, R.A. 1995. The South Dakota Breeding Bird Atlas. South Dakota Ornithologists' Union. Aberdeen, SD. 276pp.

Revised Master Economic Use Plan. 1949. Waubay NWR, Refuge files.

Ruttner, F. 1953. Fundamentals of limnology. Univ. of Toronto Press, Toronto, Ont. 242 pp.

Sample, D.W., and M.J. Mossman. 1997. Managing habitat for Grassland Birds: A Guide for Wisconsin. Bureau of Integrated Science Services. Department of Natural Resources. Madison, WI. 154 pp.

Samson, F.B. 1980. Island biogeography and the conservation of nongame birds. *Am. Wildl. Nat. Resour. Conf.* 45:245-251.

Sauer, J. R., Hines, J. E., Gough, G., Thomas, I., and B.G. Peterjohn. 1997. The North American breeding bird survey results and analysis. Version 96.3 Patuxent Wildlife Research Center, Laurel, MD.

Seastedt, T. R., and A. C. Knapp. 1993. Consequences of Nonequillibrium Resource Availability Across Multiple Time Scales: The Transient Maxima Hypothesis. *Am. Nat.* 141: 621-633.

Skinner, R.M., T.S. Baskett, and M.D. Blendon. 1984. Bird Habitat on Missouri Prairies. Missouri Department of Conservation. Terrestrial Series. 14.37pp.

South Dakota Department of Game, Fish, and Parks. 1994. Natural Heritage Database for Day County. Pierre, SD. 4 pp.

South Dakota Department of Game, Fish, and Parks. 2001. Art Smith, Compiler. 2000 Annual Report. Big Game Harvest Projections. SD Game Report. No.2001-01. Pierre, SD. 80pp.

South Dakota Ornithologists' Union, 1991. The Birds of South Dakota, 2nd Edition. NSU Press, Aberdeen, SD. 411 pp.

State Lakes Preservation Committee. 1977. A Plan for the classification, preservation, and restoration of lakes in Northeastern South Dakota. Pierre, SD.

Steinauer, E. M. and S. L. Collins. 1996. Prairie ecology - the tallgrass prairie. In Samson, F.B. and F. L. Knopf eds, Prairie Conservation Preserving North America's Most Endangered Ecosystem. Island Press, Washington, D.C. 339 pp.

Thanapura, P. 1998. Spatial modeling the initial stocking rates of cattle grazing for the Waubay National Wildlife Refuge, Day County, South Dakota. M.S. Thesis, South Dakota State University. 76p.

Tiner, R.W. 1984. Wetlands of the United States: Current status and recent trends. U.S.. Fish & Wildlife Service. U.S. Government. Printing Office, Washington D.C. 59 pp

U.S. Department of the Interior. 1988. The impacts of federal programs on wetlands. Washington D.C. 114 pp.

U.S. Fish & Wildlife Service. 1988. Birds of Waubay. Pamphlet.

U.S. Fish & Wildlife Service. 1990. Wetlands action plan. Washington, D.C. 31pp.

U.S. Fish & Wildlife Service. 1993. Western Prairie Fringed Orchid Recovery Plan, Draft.

U.S. Fish & Wildlife Service. 1996. Quick Facts from the 1996 National Survey of Fishing, Hunting, and Wildlife. Associated Recreation Pamphlet.

U.S. Fish & Wildlife Service. 1999. Waterfowl Breeding Population and Habitat Survey for South and North Dakota.

U.S. Fish & Wildlife Service. 2000. Dakota Tallgrass Prairies Habitat Preservation Area Environmental Assessment. U.S. Fish & Wildlife Service, Lakewood, CO. 31 pp.

U.S. Fish & Wildlife Service. 2000. Migratory nongame birds of management concern in the United States: the 2000 list (Draft). Office of Migratory Bird Management, Washington, D.C. 22 pp.

Vander Zouwen, W.J. 1983. Waterfowl use and habitat changes of a refuge in southern Wisconsin:1947-1980. M.S. Thesis, University of Wisconsin, Madison.

Vickery, P.D., M.L. Hunter, Jr., and S.M. Melvin. 1994. Effects of habitat area on the distribution of grassland birds in Maine. *Conservation Biology* 8:1087-1097.

Volkert, W.K. 1992. Response of grassland birds to a large scale prairie planting project. *Passenger Pigeon* 54:190-196.

Weller, M.W. 1981. Estimating wildlife and wetland losses due to drainage and other perturbations. In B. Richardson [ed] selected proceedings of the Midwest conference on wetland values and management. MN Water Planning Board. St Paul. 337-346 pp.

Westin, F.C., and D.D. Malo. 1978. Soils of South Dakota. Agriculture Experiment Station, SDSU, Bulletin 656.

Wilcove, D. 1985. Nest predation in forest tracts and the decline of migratory songbirds. *Ecology* 66:1211-1214

Wilson, S.D., and J.W. Belcher. 1989. Plant and bird communities of native prairie and introduced Eurasian vegetation in Manitoba, Canada. *Conserv. Biol.* 3:39-44

Winham, R.P. 1983. Report of a Cultural Resources Survey of an Underground Power Line Installation at the Waubay National Wildlife Refuge. Archaeology Laboratory, Center for Western Studies, Augustana College, Sioux Falls, SD.

Yahner, R.H., and P.P. Scott. 1988. Effects of forest fragmentation on depredation of artificial nests. *Journal of Wildlife Management.* 52:158-161

Zimmerman, L.J., L. Werner, L. Park, and J. Trudehope. 1978. A cultural resources survey of proposed construction sites at six U.S. Fish & Wildlife Service Refuges in South Dakota. Contract Completion Studies 56. University of South Dakota, Archaeology Laboratory. Prepared for the U.S. Fish & Wildlife Service, Pierre, SD.

Appendix C. Section 7

INTRA-SERVICE SECTION 7 BIOLOGICAL EVALUATION FORM

Originating Persons: Larry Martin, Project Leader
Bridget McCann, Refuge Planner

Telephone Numbers: (605) 947-4521; (303) 236-8145

Date: July 29, 2002

I. Region 6

II. Service Activity (Program):   Refuges & Wildlife, Waubay National Wildlife Refuge Complex
(Refuge and Wetland Management District)

III. Pertinent Species and Habitat:

A. Listed species and/or their critical habitat within the action area:

Bald eagle, *Haliaeetus leucocephalus* (threatened and proposed delisting)
Whooping crane, *Grus americana* (endangered)
Eskimo curlew, *Numenius borealis* (endangered)
Interior least tern, *Sterna antillarum* (endangered)
Piping plover, *Charadrius melodus* (threatened)
American burying beetle, *Nicrophorus americanus* (endangered)
Topeka shiner, *Notropis topeka* (endangered)
Western prairie fringed orchid, *Platanthera praeclara* (threatened)

There is no federally designated critical habitat in the action area (Waubay NWR Complex)

B. Proposed species and/or proposed critical habitat within the action area:

None

C. Candidate species within the action area:

Dakota skipper, *Hesperia dacotae*

IV Geographic area or station name and action:

Station: Waubay National Wildlife Refuge Complex in northeast South Dakota
Action: Implementation of the Comprehensive Conservation Plan for Waubay NWR Complex

V   Location:

A.   Ecoregion Number and Name: Waubay NWR Complex is located within the Service's Region 6, Mountain-Prairie Region, and specifically in the Main Stem Missouri River Ecosystem

B.   County and State: Marshall, Roberts, Day, Grant, Clark, and Codington counties, South Dakota

C.   Species/habitat occurrence:

Bald eagle: An uncommon migrant throughout South Dakota. Previously seen only during migration in Waubay WMD, but pairs have been found nesting in Roberts and Marshall counties during the last 3 years.

Piping plover: Locally common resident in the Missouri River Valley; but an uncommon migrant elsewhere in the state, including the Complex. Have rarely nested in Day and Codington counties, with the last known nesting attempt in Day County occurring in 1985.

Whooping crane: Rarely passes through the Complex during migration. Most recent sighting was in Clark County in fall of 2000.

Eskimo curlew: Not known to exist on Complex. Nearly extinct. Passes through Great Plains during migration. Could potentially occur in wet meadows within the Complex.

Interior least tern: Uncommon migrant on Complex. Nests along Missouri River in central South Dakota.

American burying beetle: Trapline on Refuge in 1996 produced no beetles. Other recent trappings have found the beetle in extreme south central South Dakota.

Topeka shiner: Not known to exist on the Complex. Recent surveys have found healthy populations in many of the tributaries of the James, Vermillion and Big Sioux Rivers.

Dakota skipper: Found on the Refuge and on some WPAs in Marshall, Roberts and Grant counties. Also found on a number of prairie sites on private and tribal lands within the WMD. Seem to be found wherever there is fairly healthy native prairie.

Western prairie fringed orchid: No known populations on the Complex. Appears to have been extirpated from South Dakota, but remote populations may have been overlooked as it does occur in adjacent counties in Minnesota, North Dakota, Iowa, and Nebraska. Occurs in moist, tallgrass prairies and sedge meadows.

VI Description of proposed action

The proposed action is the implementation of a Comprehensive Conservation Plan for Waubay NWR Complex over the next 15 years. Implementation of this Plan comprises implementation of all actions and activities to achieve the stated goals. Briefly, the CCP emphasizes the restoration, protection, and management of native grasslands, wetlands, and native woodlands. For a detailed description of proposed management objectives and strategies, please refer to the Management Direction chapter of the Draft CCP, pages 45 - 84.

VII Determination of effects:

A. Explanation of effects of the action on species and critical habitats in items III. A, B & C

Eskimo curlew, American burying beetle, Topeka shiner, Western prairie fringed orchid:

These species do not occur on the Complex. The CCP calls for protection, restoration, and management of habitats that could be used by these species; thus, the CCP will have a beneficial effect on these species should they again utilize Service lands on the Complex. None of the proposed actions in the CCP will have detrimental effects on these species or their habitats.

Bald eagle, piping plover, whooping crane, interior least tern:

These species are occasional migrants on the Complex. The bald eagle nests in very small numbers in two counties within the Complex. The other species are not known to nest on any Complex lands. The CCP calls for continued protection, restoration, and management of habitats used by these species; thus, implementing the CCP will have a beneficial effect on these species. None of the proposed actions in the CCP will have detrimental effects on these species or their habitats.

Dakota skipper:

This species does occur on the Refuge and in the WMD on sites with healthy native prairie. The CCP calls for continued protection, restoration, and management of prairie habitat. Thus, implementing the CCP will have a beneficial effect on this species. Prescribed fire could adversely affect this species if conducted on too large of an area all at once. However, actions will be taken to avoid this impact. None of the other proposed actions in the CCP will have detrimental effects on this species or its habitat.

There is no federally designated critical habitat on the action area (Waubay NWR Complex) nor is there a need to propose designating critical habitat within the Refuge

B. Explanation of actions to be implemented to reduce adverse effects:
In order to protect the Dakota skipper and its habitat, management units on which it is found will be divided into smaller sub-units to prevent management activities, such as burning or haying, from affecting the whole unit all at once.

VIII Effect determination and response requeste[* = optional]

A. Listed species/designated critical habitat:

Determination	Response requested
no effect/no adverse modification (Species: Eskimo curlew, American burying beetle, Topeka shiner, Western prairie fringed orchid)	_____ *Concurrence
may affect, but is not likely to adversely affect species/adversely modify critical habitat (Species: Bald eagle, piping plover, whooping crane, interior least tern)	_____ Concurrence
may affect, and is likely to adversely affect species /adversely modify critical habitat (species: NONE)	_____ Formal Consultation

B. Proposed species/proposed critical habitat

Determination	Response requested
no effect on proposed species/no adverse modification of proposed critical habitat (species: NONE)	_____ *Concurrence
Is likely to jeopardize proposed species/ adversely modify proposed critical habitat (species: NONE)	_____ Conference

C. Candidate Species:

Determination	Response requested
no effect	_____ *Concurrence
(Species: NONE)	
may affect, not likely to jeopardize the species	_____ Concurrence
(Species: Dakota skipper)	
is likely to jeopardize candidate species	_____ Conference
(species: NONE)	

_____   7/31/02
Larry Martin, Project Leader,   Date
Waubay National Wildlife Refuge Complex

IX Reviewing ESO Evaluation:

A. Concurrence __X__   Nonconcurrence _____

B. Formal Consultation required: _____

C. Conference required: _____

D. Informal conference required: _____

E. Remarks:

_____   8-12-02
Donald Gober   Date
South Dakota Field Supervisor, U.S. Fish & Wildlife Service

Appendix D. Glossary

Anadromous: Fish which swim up rivers from the sea at certain seasons for breeding (i.e. salmon).

Animal Impact: Sum total of all direct physical influences of livestock on grasslands such as trampling, dunging, urinating, salivating, rubbing, digging, etc. Animal impact is controlled through stock density and time.

Animal Unit Month (AUM): An AUM is the amount of forage necessary to maintain one 1,000-pound animal for 1 month.

Brood water: Wetlands with semipermanent or permanent water regimes used by ducks for the rearing and protection of ducklings.

Conservation Reserve Program(CRP): A Department of Agriculture program where payments are made to landowners to idle cropland.

Cool Season Exotic Grasses: Cool season grasses introduced to the Waubay Complex. They include smooth brome, quack grass, Kentucky bluegrass, intermediate wheatgrass, and tall wheatgrass.

Cool Season Grasses: These grasses have a C_3 photosynthetic process. Optimum growth of cool season grasses is approximately 65-75 °F. In the Waubay Complex, their primary growth periods are spring and fall. Examples include green needle grass, smooth brome, western wheatgrass, intermediate wheatgrass, and needle-and-thread.

Dense Nesting Cover (DNC): A combination of grasses and legumes planted to provide tall dense cover. DNC describes cover planted for upland nesting waterfowl in the Prairie Pothole Region. Principal species of vegetation used in DNC mixes include tall wheatgrass, intermediate wheatgrass, alfalfa, and sweet clover. This mix of species provides the necessary structural components for tall, upright residual vegetation.

Deteriorated (poor condition): As applied to grasslands in this EA, refers to a condition of less-than-potential total biotic productivity. Low productivity is usually the result of environmental conditions not natural to the site. Deteriorated grasslands typically have low species diversity (plant and animal), poor plant vigor, and significant proportions of undesirable plant species.

Duck Stamp: Common name for Migratory Bird Hunting and Conservation Stamp. Purchased by hunters and others to fund land purchases for migratory bird conservation.

Endangered: A plant or animal species listed under the Endangered Species Act that is in danger of extinction throughout all or a significant portion of its range.

Endemic Species: Plants or animals that occur naturally in a certain region and whose distribution is relatively limited to a particular locality.

Eutrophication: The process of a lake aging caused by nutrient enrichment, resulting in increased production and deposition of organic matter.

Extirpated: no longer existing in area, wiped out, locally extinct.

Fee-title: Lands owned by the U.S. Fish & Wildlife Service.

Fauna: All the vertebrate and invertebrate animals of an area.

Flora: All the plant species of an area.

Forb: A broad-leaved, herbaceous plant; for example, a columbine.

Grazing: Livestock feeding on grasses and herbage.

Grassland Succession: Natural process of change and development in the entire grassland communities.

Haying: Mechanical removal of grasses and herbage for livestock feed.

High Succession: Complex communities composed of populations of many different species of plants, animals, birds, insects, and microorganisms. Usually highly stable and not prone to high fluctuations in numbers of individual populations.

High Grassland Succession: Complex grassland communities composed of populations of a great many different species of plants, animals, birds, insects, and micro-organisms. Usually highly stable and not prone to high fluctuations in numbers of individual populations.

Indigenous: Occurring or living naturally in a geographic area.

Indigenous Migratory Birds: Migratory birds occurring or living naturally within the Waubay Complex. Synonymous with native species.

Insectivore: mammals depending on insects as food. For example - moles, shrews.

Integrated Pest Management (IPM): Control of pests utilizing a practical, economical, and scientifically based combination of biological, physical, cultural, and chemical control methods. IPM emphasizes these methods in order to reduce or eliminate the need for chemical pesticides. It is a balanced approach which considers hazard to the environment, efficacy, cost, and vulnerability of pests.

Legumes: Any of a large family of plants including peas, beans, and clovers that are used for food and forage, bearing nodules on the roots that contain nitrogen-fixing bacteria.

Litter: Residual vegetation which has lodged and become matted.

Low Succession: Simple communities composed of populations of only a few species. Usually highly unstable and vulnerable to fluctuations.

Low Grassland Succession: Simple grassland communities composed of populations of only a few species. Usually highly unstable and vulnerable to fluctuations.

Macroinvertebrate: larger invertebrates, animals without a backbone.

Migratory birds: Birds which follow a seasonal movement from their breeding grounds to their "wintering" grounds. Waterfowl, shorebirds, raptors, and song birds are all migratory birds.

Mowing: Mechanical cutting of grasses and herbage <u>without</u> the removal of the cut grasses and herbage.

Neotropical Migrant: A bird species that breeds north of the U.S./Mexican border and winters primarily south of this border.

Noxious Weed: A plant species designated by Federal or State law as generally possessing one or more of the following characteristics: aggressive or difficult to manage; parasitic; a carrier or host of serious insect or disease; or nonnative, new, or not common to the United States. According to the Federal Noxious Weed Act (PL 93-639), a noxious weed is one that causes disease or had adverse effects on man or his environment and, therefore, is detrimental to the agriculture and commerce of the Untied States and to the public health.

Obligate hydrophyte: Species that are found only in wetlands, such as cattails.

Overwater Nesting: Method of using wetland vegetation to build a nest that floats on water; used by migratory birds such as canvasback ducks, ruddy ducks, and grebes.

Passerine: Perching songbird; order includes over half of all birds. For example - sparrows, finches, warblers.

Perpetual: Continuing forever, permanent.

Prescribed Burn: Controlled application of fire to wildland fuels in either their natural or modified state. Fire is confined to a predetermined area while producing heat intensity and rate of spread required to achieve planned management objectives.

Residual Vegetation: Upright dead vegetation remaining from previous years of growth. Residual vegetation is different from litter in that it has not lodged.

Revenue Sharing Trust Fund: A fund provided to the County to offset the difference between taxes and revenue sharing. The amount of the fund is set so that interest earned yearly on this principal would provide the shortfall amount.

Succession: Process of change and development in community components—soil, micro-organisms, animal and plant life and microenvironment.

Seeded Nesting Cover: Vegetation planted to provide nesting cover, usually cover planted for upland nesting waterfowl in the Prairie Pothole Region. This may include DNC, cool and warm season grasses, forbs, and shrubs.

Small Wetlands Acquisition Program(SWAP): U.S. Fish & Wildlife Service program used to purchase easements and fee-title land to protect wetlands.

Tame Grass Plantings: Planted vegetation, typically a monotypic planting of a single cool season exotic grass such as smooth brome, intermediate wheatgrass, or crested wheatgrass. A legume, usually alfalfa, may be planted with a grass.

Warm Season Grasses: These grasses have a C_4 photosynthetic process. Optimum growth of warm season grasses is approximately 90 to 95 °F. In the Waubay Complex, their primary growth periods are in the summer. Examples include switchgrass, big bluestem, little bluestem, and sideoats grama.

Waterbank: A Department of Agriculture program where payments are made to landowners to protect wetlands and uplands associated with these wetlands.

Waubay Complex: Includes both the National Wildlife Refuge and the Wetland Management District.

Wetland Reserve Program(WRP): A Department of Agriculture program where payments are made to landowners to protect wetlands and uplands associated with these wetlands.

Winterkill: When dissolved oxygen levels drop to a point which cannot support large fish species.

Appendix E. Acronyms

ARPA - Archaeological Resources Protection Act
BBS - Breeding Bird Survey
CCP - Comprehensive Conservation Plan
CEA - Conservation Extension Agreement
COE - Corps of Engineers
CRP - Conservation Reserve Program
DTP-WMA - Dakota Tallgrass Prairie Wildlife Mgmt. Area
EA -Environmental Assessment
FmHA - Farmers Home Administration
GIS - Geographic Information Systems
GPS - Global Positioning System
HAPET - Habitat and Population Evaluation Team
HMP - Habitat Management Plan
IPM - Integrated Pest Management
LWCF - Land and Water Conservation Fund
NHPA - National Historic Preservation Act
NWR - National Wildlife Refuge
NWRS - National Wildlife Refuge System
NRHP - National Register of Historic Places
PFW - Partners for Fish and Wildlife
PPR - Prairie Pothole Region
PUMR - Public Use Minimum Requirement
SD GF&P - South Dakota Game, Fish and Parks
SUP - Special Use Permit
SWAP - Small Wetlands Acquisition Program
TNC - The Nature Conservancy
USDA - United States Department of Agriculture
USFWS - U.S. Fish & Wildlife Service
WBPD map - Waterfowl Breeding Pair Distribution
WEA - Wildlife Extension Agreement
WMD - Wetland Management District
WPA - Waterfowl Production Area
WRP - Wetland Reserve Program
WWPP - Waubay Watershed Protection Project

Appendix F. Key Legislation/ Policies

Volunteer and Partnership Enhancement Act of 1998: To amend the Fish and Wildlife Act of 1956 to promote volunteer programs and community partnerships for the benefit of national wildlife refuges, and for other purposes. October 5, 1998

Executive Order 13084, Consultation and Coordination With Indian Tribal Governments (1998): The United States has a unique legal relationship with Indian tribal governments as set forth in the Constitution of the United States, treaties, statutes, Executive orders, and court decisions. Since the formation of the Union, the United States has recognized Indian tribes as domestic dependent nations under its protection. In treaties, our Nation has guaranteed the right of Indian tribes to self-government. As domestic dependent nations, Indian tribes exercise inherent sovereign powers over their members and territory. The United States continues to work with Indian tribes on a government-to-government basis to address issues concerning Indian tribal self-government, trust resources, and Indian tribal treaty and other rights.

National Wildlife Refuge System Improvement Act of 1997: Sets the mission and administrative policy for all refuges in the National Wildlife Refuge System. Clearly defines a unifying mission for the Refuge System; establishes the legitimacy and appropriateness of the six priority public uses (hunting, fishing, wildlife observation, wildlife photography, environmental education and interpretation); establishes a formal process for determining compatibility; establishes the responsibilities of the Secretary of the Interior for managing and protecting the System; and requires a Comprehensive Conservation Plan for each refuge by the year 2012. This Act amended portions of the Refuge Recreation Act and National Wildlife Refuge System Administration Act of 1966.

Executive Order 13007 Indian Sacred Sites (1996): Directs Federal land management agencies to accommodate access to and ceremonial use of Indian sacred sites by Indian religious practitioners, avoid adversely affecting the physical integrity of such sacred sites, and where appropriate, maintain the confidentiality of sacred sites.

Executive Order 12996 Management and General Public Use of the National Wildlife Refuge System (1996): Defines the mission, purpose, and priority public uses of the National Wildlife Refuge System. It also presents four principles to guide management of the System.

Americans With Disabilities Act (1992): Prohibits discrimination in public accommodations and services

Native American Graves Protection and Repatriation Act (1990): Requires Federal agencies and museums to inventory, determine ownership of, and repatriate cultural items under their control or possession.

Federal Noxious Weed Act (1990): Requires the use of integrated management systems to control or contain undesirable plant species; and an interdisciplinary approach with the cooperation of other Federal and State agencies.

North American Wetlands Conservation Act of December 13, 1989 (16 U.S.C. 4401-4412): Public Law 101-233 provides funding and administrative direction for implementation of the North American Waterfowl Management Plan and the Tripartite Agreement on wetlands between Canada, U.S. and Mexico.

Agricultural Credit Act of 1987, Public Law 100-233: Authorizes the Farmer's Home Administration to transfer fee-title or assign interests in real estate to the U.S. Fish & Wildlife Service for the protection of floodplains, wetlands, and surrounding uplands.

Emergency Wetlands Resources Act (1986): The purpose of the Act is "To promote the conservation of migratory waterfowl and to offset or prevent the serious loss of wetlands by the acquisition of wetlands and other essential habitat, and for other purposes."

Food Security Act of 1985 (Title XII, Public Law 99-198, 99 Stat. 1354; December 23, 1985), as amended: This Act authorizes acquisition of easements in real property for a term of not less than 50 years for conservation, recreation, and wildlife purposes.

Farmland Protection Policy Act of 1980 and 1995: Requires identification of proposed actions that would affect any lands classified as prime and unique farmlands. The U.S. Natural Resources Conservation Service (formerly Soil Conservation Service) administers this act to preserve farmland. Contact the U.S. Natural Resources Conservation Service office in the project area and ask them to determine if the proposed action will affect any lands classified as prime and unique farmlands.

Archaeological Resources Protection Act (1979) as amended: Protects materials of archaeological interest from unauthorized removal or destruction and requires Federal managers to develop plans and schedules to locate archaeological resources.

American Indian Religious Freedom Act (1978): Directs agencies to consult with native traditional religious leaders to determine appropriate policy changes necessary to protect and preserve Native American religious cultural rights and practices.

Executive Order 11990, Protection of Wetlands (1977): This order directs all Federal agencies to avoid, if possible, adverse impacts to wetlands and to preserve and enhance the natural and beneficial values of wetlands. Each agency shall avoid undertaking or assisting in wetland construction projects unless the head of the agency determines that there is no practicable alternative to such construction and that the proposed action includes measures to minimize harm. Also, agencies shall provide opportunity for early public review of proposals for construction in wetlands, including those projects not requiring an EIS.

Executive Order 11988, Floodplain Management (1977): Each Federal agency shall provide leadership and take action to reduce the risk of flood loss and minimize the impact of floods on human safety, and preserve the natural and beneficial values served by the floodplains.

Executive Order 11987, Exotic Organisms (1977): This Executive Order requires Federal agencies, to the extent permitted by law, to: restrict the introduction of exotic species into the natural ecosystems on lands and waters owned or leased by the United States; encourage States, local governments, and private citizens to prevent the introduction of exotic species into natural ecosystems of the U.S.; restrict the importation and introduction of exotic species into any natural U.S. ecosystems as a result of activities they undertake, fund, or authorize; and restrict the use of Federal funds, programs, or authorities to export native species for introduction into ecosystems outside the U.S. where they do not occur naturally.

Clean Water Act (1977): Requires consultation with the Corps of Engineers (404 permits) for major wetland modifications.

Archaeological and Historic Preservation Act (1974): Directs the preservation of historic and archaeological data in Federal construction projects.

Rehabilitation Act (1973): Requires programmatic accessibility in addition to physical accessibility for all facilities and programs funded by the Federal government to ensure that anybody can participate in any program.

Endangered Species Act (1973): Requires all Federal agencies to carry out programs for the conservation of endangered and threatened species.

Executive Order 11644, Use of Off-road Vehicles on Public Lands (1972): Defines zones of use by off-road vehicles on public lands.

Wild and Scenic Rivers Act (1972): This Act establishes a National Wild and Scenic Rivers System for the protection of rivers with important scenic, recreational, fish and wildlife, and other values. Rivers are classified as wild, scenic or recreational. The Act designates specific rivers for inclusion in the System and prescribes the methods and standards by which additional rivers may be added. The Act contains procedures and limitations for control of lands in federally administered components of the System and for disposition of lands and minerals under Federal ownership. Hunting and fishing are permitted in components of the System under applicable Federal and state laws.

National Environmental Policy Act (1969): Requires the disclosure of the environmental impacts of any major Federal action significantly affecting the quality of the human environment.

Architectural Barriers Act (1968): Requires federally owned, leased, or funded buildings and facilities to be accessible to persons with disabilities.

National Historic Preservation Act (1966) as amended: Establishes as policy that the Federal Government is to provide leadership in the preservation of the nation's prehistoric and historic resources.

National Wildlife Refuge System Administration Act of 1966 as amended by the National Wildlife Refuge System Improvement Act of 1997, 16 U.S.C. 668dd-668ee. (Refuge Administration Act): Defines the National Wildlife Refuge System and authorizes the Secretary to permit any use of a refuge provided such use is compatible with the major purposes for which the refuge was established. The Refuge Improvement Act clearly defines a unifying mission for the Refuge System; establishes the legitimacy and appropriateness of the six priority public uses (hunting, fishing, wildlife observation, wildlife photography, environmental education and interpretation); establishes a formal process for determining compatibility; established the responsibilities of the Secretary of Interior for managing and protecting the System; and requires a Comprehensive Conservation Plan for each refuge by the year 2012. This Act amended portions of the Refuge Recreation Act and National Wildlife Refuge System Administration Act of 1966.

Land and Water Conservation Fund Act (1965): Uses the receipts from the sale of surplus Federal land, outer continental shelf oil and gas sales, and other sources for land acquisition under several authorities.

Refuge Recreation Act (1962): Allows the use of refuges for recreation when such uses are compatible with the refuge's primary purposes and when sufficient funds are available to manage the uses.

Fish and Wildlife Act (1956): Established a comprehensive national fish and wildlife policy and broadened the authority for acquisition and development of refuges.

Federal Aid in Fish Restoration Act of August 9, 1950 (16 U.S.C. 777-777k), as amended: This Act, commonly referred to as the "Dingell-Johnson Act," provides aid to the States for management and restoration of fish having material value in connection with sport or recreation in marine or fresh waters. Funds from an excise tax on certain items of sport fishing tackle are appropriated to the Secretary of Interior annually and apportioned to States on a formula basis for approved land acquisition, research, development and management projects.

Bald and Golden Eagle Protection Act (1940): The Act prohibits the taking or possession of and commerce in bald and golden eagles, with limited exceptions. The enacting clause of the original Act stated that the Continental Congress in 1782 adopted the bald eagle as the national symbol; that the bald eagle became the symbolic representation of a new nation and the American ideals of freedom; and that the bald eagle threatened with extinction.

Federal Aid in Wildlife Restoration Act of September 2, 1937 (16 U.S.C. 669-669i), as amended: This Act, commonly referred to as the "Pittman-Robertson Act," provides to States for game and nongame wildlife restoration work. Funds from an excise tax on sporting arms and ammunition are appropriated to the Secretary of the Interior annually and apportioned to States on a formula basis for approved land acquisition, research, development and management projects and hunter safety programs.

Migratory Bird Hunting and Conservation Stamp Act (1934): Authorized the opening of part of a refuge to waterfowl hunting. Also authorized the acquisition of Waterfowl Production Areas (WPAs) through both fee-title and easements.

Fish and Wildlife Coordination Act of March 10, 1934 (16 U.S.C. 661-66c), as amended: This Act authorizes the Secretary of the Interior to assist Federal, State and other agencies in development, protection, rearing and stocking fish and wildlife on Federal lands, and to study effects of pollution on fish and wildlife. The Act also requires consultation with the U.S. Fish & Wildlife Service and the wildlife agency of any State wherein the waters of any stream or other water body are proposed to be impounded, diverted, channelized or otherwise controlled or modified by any Federal agency, or any private agency under Federal permit or license, with a view to preventing loss of, or damage to, wildlife resources in connection with such water resource projects. The Act further authorizes Federal water resource agencies to acquire lands or interests in connection with water use projects specifically for mitigation and enhancement of fish and wildlife.

Migratory Bird Conservation Act (1929): Establishes procedures for acquisition by purchase, rental, or gift of areas approved by the Migratory Bird Conservation Commission.

Migratory Bird Treaty Act (1918): Designates the protection of migratory birds as a Federal responsibility. This Act enables the setting of seasons, and other regulations including the closing of areas, Federal or non-Federal, to the hunting of migratory birds.

Antiquities Act (1906): Authorizes the scientific investigation of antiquities on Federal land and provides penalties for unauthorized removal of objects taken or collected without a permit.

Appendix G. Mailing List

Federal Officials
- Senator Tom Daschle, Washington, D.C. and Aberdeen, SD (Beth Smith)
- Senator Tim Johnson, Washington, D.C. and Aberdeen, SD (Sharon Stroschein)
- Representative John Thune, Washington, D.C. and Aberdeen, SD (Mark Vaux)

Federal Agencies
- US Army Corps of Engineers; Steven Naler
- US Department of Agriculture
  APHIS-PPQ, Bruce Helbig
  Farm Service Agency
    (Paul Hanson, Clark Co.; W. Stanley Lamb, Codington Co.; Donna Beitelspacher, Day Co.; Joel Foster, Grant Co.; Stan Thompson, Marshall Co.; Curtis Sylte, Roberts Co.; Steven Cutler, State Executive Director)
  Natural Resource Conservation Service
    (Earl Henderson, Clark Co.; Arlene Brandt-Jensen, Codington Co.; Ron Christianson, Day Co.; Dale Johnson, Grant Co.; Tom Martin, Marshall Co.; Kent Duerre, Roberts Co.; Connie Vicuna, Biologist; Janet Oertly, State Conservationist)
- US EPA, Denver, CO
- US Fish & Wildlife Service: Denver, CO; Arlington, VA; Portland, OR; Albuquerque, NM; Anchorage, AK; Juneau, AK; Fort Snelling, MN; Atlanta, GA; Hadley, MA; Sacramento, CA; Shepherdstown, WV; Sherwood, OR; Air Quality Branch, Lakewood, CO; Tewaukon NWR, ND; Lost Trail NWR, MT; Medicine Lake NWR, MT; Crescent Lake/North Platte NWR, NE; Arrowwood NWR, ND; Sand Lake NWR, SD; Alamosa/ Monte Vista NWR, CO; Arapaho NWR, CO; Ecological Services - Pierre, SD; Big Stone NWR, MN; Morris WMD, MN; Madison WMD, SD; Huron WMD, SD; Lacreek NWR, SD; Brookings WHO, SD; Lake Andes NWR, SD
- US Geological Survey (Rick Benson; Dr. Charles Berry, SDSU Coop. Wildlife Research Unit; Doug Johnson, Northern Prairie Science Center; Rick Schroeder, Midcontinent Ecological Service Center)

Tribal Officials
- Sisseton Wahpeton Sioux Tribe - Fish and Wildlife Department, Alvah Quinn

State Officials
- Governor William J. Janklow
- Representatives (Tim Begalka; Art Fryslie; Gary Hanson; Claire Konold; Jim Peterson; David Sigestad; Jim Hundstad; Al Koistinen; Duane Sutton)
- Senators (Don Brosz; H. Paul Dennert; Larry Diedrich; Brock Greenfield; Paul Symens)

State Agencies
- Department of Agriculture - Ron Moehring
- Department of Environment and Natural Resources - John Hatch, P.E.
- Department of Game, Fish and Parks (John Cooper, Secretary; Doug Alvine, Regional Supervisor, Watertown; Ron Meester, Fisheries Manager, Webster; Paul Coughlin, Senior Wetlands Biologist, Pierre; SD Game, Fish and Parks Commissioners: Tim Kessler, Chairman)
- Department of Military & Veterans Affairs - Division of Emergency Management; Gary Whitney
- SD State Historical Society
- Illinois Department of Natural Resources - Tom Nelson

City/County/Local Governments
- 1st Dist. Assoc. of Local Govt. - Gregory Maag
- Fort Township - John Hogland, Chairman
- Grant Co. Commissioners
- Marshall Co. Commissioners
- Roberts Co. Commissioners
- Codington Co. Commissioners
- Clark Co. Commissioners
- Day Co. Commissioners
- Watertown City - Mayor Brenda Barger
- Waubay City - Mayor Kevin Jens
- Webster City - Mayor Mike Grosek

Libraries
- Webster Public Library
- Britton Public Library
- Watertown Public Library
- Waubay Public Library
- Grant County Public Library
- Emil M. Larson Public Library
- Sisseton Memorial Library

Organizations
- Animal Protection Institute, Sacramento, CA
- Chambers of Commerce - Milbank, Watertown, Sisseton, Webster
- Clark Co. Pro Pheasants - Fred Obemeier
- Conservation Districts (Diane Bowers, Clark Co.; Sandy Law, Codington Co.; Noel Anderson; Dennis Skadsen, Project Coord.; Day Co.; Jan Berger, Grant Co.; Wanda Franzen, Marshall Co.; June Helgeson, Roberts Co.)
- Defenders of Wildlife - Noah Matson; Tom Uniack
- Ducks Unlimited, Inc. - Rick Warhurst, Bismarck
- EDWDD, Jay Gilbertson
- Farm Bureau of SD - Richard Kjerstad, President
- Girl Scouts of America (Service Center, Marian Raml; Webster Troop 4004, Marianna Finn)
- Glacial Lakes and Prairies Tourism Assoc.
- Institute for Policy Research - H. Paul Friesema
- Izaak Walton League - James Madsen
- Klein Family Farms, Inc. - Earl Monnens
- KRA Corporation, F&W Reference Service
- National Audubon Society - Gretchen Muller
- National Farmers Organization - Dave Meyer, President
- National Trappers Association - Scott Hartman
- National Wildlife Refuge Assoc. - Brent Giezentanner
- The Nature Conservancy - Pete Bauman; John Humke
- Nobles County Env. Service - Judy Petersen
- North American Bluebird Society - John Ivanko and Lisa Kivirist
- Outdoor Women of SD - NE Chapter
- Phillips Petroleum Co., Laws and Regulations Department - B.D. "Diann" Beene
- Prairie Restorations, Inc. - Ron Bower

- SD BASS Federation - Phillip Risnes
- SD Ornithologists' Union
- SD Wildlife Federation - Chris Hesla
- The Wildlife Society, Central Mountain & Plains Sec.
- Upper Big Sioux River Watershed Project - Mike Williams
- Whitetail Bowman Archery Club - Bob Jensen
- The Wilderness Society
- Wildlife Management Institute - Bob Bryne (CARE); Rob Manes
- The Wildlife Society - SD Chapter; Paul Coughlin, President

Newspapers
- Aberdeen American News
- Britton Journal
- Clark County Courier
- Grant County Review
- Langford Bugle
- Sisseton Courier
- South Shore Gazette
- Reporter & Farmer, Webster
- Watertown Public Opinion
- Wilmot Enterprise

Schools/Universities
- Augustana College - Peter Winham, Archeology Lab.
- South Dakota State University - Extension Service (Chuck Tollefson, Clark Co. Ext. Agent; Chuck Langner, Codington Co. Ext. Agent; Gary Troester, Day Co. Ext. Agent; Amy Kruse, Grant Co. Ext. Agent; Lorne Tilberg, Marshall Co. Ext. Agent; Sandy Gregg, Roberts Co. Ext. Agent; Leon Wrage)
- South Shore School, Max Nawroth

Individuals

Jim Anderson
James Barnett
Richard Barnett
Kurt Bassett
Frank Bauer
Frank Benoit
Loren Berg
Art Berger
Gordon Bergquist
Neil Bien
Rory Binkerd
Douglas and Elaine Block
Craig Brown
Dan Brown
Robert Brown
Marvin Bury
Kenneth Cameron
Jeff Case
Mark Conrad
Dr. M. S. Dorsett
John Dorsett
Bruce Eldridge
Maurice Erickson
Calvin Finnesand
Lylas Fisher
Donald Foote
Byron E. Foreman
Dennis Foster
Ms. Dorothy Foster
Kevin Fridley
Chuck Fromelt
Charles Fulker
Charles Gauker
Delton Gerber
Derek Greene
Duaine Greenhagen
Robert Gruba
Harlan Hagen
Harold Hansen
Bruce Harris
Robert Hartinger
Frank Heidelbauer
Clinton Hellevang
Scott Helms
James Hendrickson
Dale Henry
Orlin Jameson
The Johnsons
Gary Jongeling
C.M. Keintz
Kim Kempton
Margaret King
Dean Kirkeby
Roger Knapp
LeRon Knebel
Alfred LaMee
Scott Larson
Loriann Lindner
Ron Loeschke
Don Mahlen
Jerry Marnette
Gary Marrone
Bob Martenson
Joy McGregor
Kim McWilliams
John K. Miller
Mac Miller
James O. Monson
Rick Norris
William Obermeier

Lela Olson
Dr. Jason Ostby
Kermit Parks
Ben Parsons
Vernon Pearson
Ken Pigors
Tim Pravecek
Thomas L. Raines
Mark Redlinger
Ken Rock
Lester Rowland
Sam Rudolph
Herbert Samson
Allen Sass
Jerry Schlosser
Steven Schultz
Larry Schwarze
Robert Sommers
Loy Stange
Duane Steege
David Strang
Orman Street
William Street
Lowell Summa
Jim Sweeting
David Trautner
Jerry Travis
Tony Travis
Bob Urevig
David Wade
Daniel M. Weber
Henry L. Wells
Robert F. Witt
John Woodman
Dennis Zenk
Fred Zenk

Appendix H. WPA Management Priorities

Waubay Wetland Management District includes a diverse group of 199 Waterfowl Production Areas spread over six counties. Many of the WPAs were purchased in pieces from different landowners. For the sake of the discussion in this section, a WPA consists of one, or more, purchased tracts which are managed together as a unit.

The WPAs range in size from 0.98 to 1674 acres. They vary from all water to all uplands. Uplands vary from tame grasses to native grasses being dominant. Most of the WPAs are located on the Coteau Des Prairies, but there are also units in the James Basin, and Minnesota River-Red River Lowlands. Surrounding land uses range from primarily cropland to dominated by rangeland. WPAs range from being bordered by a United States Highway to being inaccessible to the general public. Some WPAs have uplands in good nesting condition and require only maintenance management, while others require aggressive management to change the current condition. There is no such thing as a "typical" WPA and all of the above factors influence the management of any individual WPA.

Many of the comments provided in the CCP public process suggested that more management (grazing, burning, haying) be done on WPAs (see Consultation and Coordination with Others). These comments echoed an annual sentiment of the staff, that there is so much more that could be done. Due to current staff and budget, only about 10 percent of WPAs are actively managed in any year. Management is done in many cases on an opportunistic basis. For example, where the previous landowner has cattle adjoining the WPA.

It is obvious from bird use of these units that all migratory birds do not view WPAs as equal. Therefore, it seemed appropriate to divide WPAs into priority groups so that more resources, time and money, could be spent on WPAs that have the greatest potential of achieving the mission of the WMD.

There are three factors that were considered in compiling the priority list. Those factors were the Waterfowl Breeding Pair Distributions Map, the size of the WPA and the upland to wetland ratio.

The Waterfowl Breeding Pair Distributions map (Map 8) shows where waterfowl breeding pairs are located. By focusing resources (time and money) on areas with an average of 25 duck pairs per square mile and above, the greatest effect can be realized.

Many studies have concluded that large tracts of grasslands are best for nesting birds, both waterfowl and passerines (Burger et al. 1994; Duebbert and Kantrud 1974; Herkert 1994; Samson 1980: Vickery et al. 1994). The highest priority was given to tracts of 160 acres or more. A medium priority was given to tracts 60 - 159 acres. The lowest priority was for tracts less then 80 acres.

The upland to wetland ratio is a management consideration based on the economy of scale concept. Wetlands are critical for waterfowl broods, but uplands are needed by most species for nesting. There is little management that can be done to wetlands, so the higher the upland to wetland ratio is, the more management potential exists. The highest priority was given to tracts with an upland to wetland ratio of at least 1. A medium priority was assigned to tracts with upland to wetland ratios of .75 - .99. A low priority was given to tracts with an upland to wetland ratio of less then .75.

Three groups of WPAs were developed. These are labeled A, B and C, with A being the highest priority. Below is a description of what specific criteria were used for each and what the management implications are:

A: These areas were selected to represent the best nesting units in the WMD. They must be a minimum of 160 acres and have a minimum upland to wetland ratio of one. "A" WPAs will be managed and monitored yearly. Sixty-one, or 31 percent, of the WPAs are in this group. Rest will be used as a management tool as needed. If previous commitments for grazing/haying have not been made, the tracts will be put out for bid. Burning is another management tool that may be used. These WPAs will be monitored to assure that dense nesting cover is being maintained. Within the A category there are some units that are good native grass stands. These will be monitored to ensure there is no loss of plant diversity or encroachment of tame or exotic vegetation. Other WPAs in this category have poor nesting cover. These units will be actively managed to alter their current condition.

B: These areas were selected if they were a minimum of 80 acres and upland to wetland ratio of .75. There are 52 tracts, or 26 percent of the WPAs, in this group. These WPAs will be managed on an opportunistic basis, as time and money permit.

C: These units will not be managed. There are 86 units in this category. Weeds will be controlled and signs maintained.

For 5 percent of the units, the category an individual WPA should have been in was changed due to manager discretion. Discretion was used when other conditions where known to exist which were not included in the original evaluation. Some units were very close to one of the cutoffs and due to the presence of grassland easement or state lands adjoining the unit it was elevated to the next level. Many of the changes were units that were placed into the "C" category for now due to current high water levels. These categories are not static. They can and will be changed if conditions change.

All counties have units within each of the categories. A complete listing follows.

PRIORITY LIST A

WPA	Acres	up/wet ratio	T-Storm score	County
Lamb (121,499)	320	1.1	50	Clark
Neal-Barton (180,452)	315.7	1.78	36	Clark
Geidd-Hagen etc. (299,375,306,469)	292.85	2.68	49.3	Clark
Markrud-Larkin (219,427)	280	1.3	43.3	Clark
Lacraft (329)	160	2.45	43	Clark
Anderson (101,a)	160	2.17	50	Clark
Bender (179)	160	1.49	47.2	Clark
Herker (471)	160	1.01	48.6	Clark
Huppler-Springer (66, 68)	777.81	2.08	29.4	Codington
Warner Lake (1,110, 133, 343, 383)	745.47	9.53	49.7	Codington
Roe E&A (107, 131, 107 b-c)	720	3.67	47.2	Codington
Horseshoe L. (Roe) (107a)	617.47	2.6	51.8	Codington
Overland-Korth (155)	390.95	4.17	48.6	Codington
Johnson (120)	297.97	2.13	36.3	Codington
Bursvold-Darling-Sandel (41,111, 158)	241.93	1.3	38.8	Codington
Thompson (12)	226.5	0.9	36	Codington
Bruflat (135)	190	1.64	36.7	Codington
Rasmussen-Moorhouse (36a,64)	185.2	1.56	36	Codington
Roe, E. (159,a)	177	3.56	50.9	Codington
Coplan (16, a)	160	1.92	36	Codington
Moe, T.D. (156)	160	1.79	25	Codington
Stangland-Augustana (25, 60)	635.2	1.82	64.4	Day
Kriech-Becht-Lanager (13, 26, 276, 296)	340	1.72	60.8	Day
Meuer-Orness (14, 19)	314.42	2.94	51.8	Day
E. Hanson-Thurow (59, 474)	280	3.5	50	Day
West Storley (56 a)	195.88	3.3	50	Day
N. Taylor-Helwig (291, 216)	180	1.36	50	Day
McCarlson-Johnson (15, 333)	179.46	1.59	50	Day
Zenk (319)	160.45	2.22	43	Day
Donat (22)	160	1.99	50	Day
S. Taylor (291 a)	160	1.66	50	Day
Hendrickson-U.S. (55, 1a)	160	1.25	43	Day
Hagen (290)	159	1.69	36	Day
O'Farrell-Reyelts (24, 148)	1674.1	5.37	67.5	Grant
Meyer Lake (149)	1325.44	1.85	59.6	Grant
Price-Kaufman (82, 85)	340	2.47	26.2	Grant
Meyer-Janssen (41, 42)	280	1.06	62.6	Grant
Berger-Eidet (73, 74)	209.17	1.33	36	Grant
VanHout (59)	160	7.81	25	Grant
Peterson-Solem (60, 61)	160	2.06	36	Grant
Jensen (274)	1100	2.27	68	Marshall
Lake Emma (22, 126, 143, 186, 231,etc.)	1069	3.36	70.7	Marshall
N. Red Iron Lake (76, 250, 272)	918.7	3.64	64.4	Marshall
Cottonwood Lk.(94, 150, 260)	851.71	2.75	55.4	Marshall
Ruckdashel-Hofland (11, 244)	804.91	4.05	68	Marshall
Lamee N. & S. (84)	762.89	4.9	60.8	Marshall
Peterson Memorial (33, 122)	640	3.74	67.1	Marshall
Deutsch (47, 2, 108, 220, 214)	612.83	1.68	54.44	Marshall
LCFJ (92, 134, 161, 249, 251)	519.93	3.97	51.8	Marshall
Abraham Lake (255, 257, 268)	466.8	5.55	49.5	Marshall
Ringer-Guy (217, 258)	419.34	3.91	51.8	Marshall
Rolstad (69, 269)	405.39	2.91	79.7	Marshall
Buss (227)	160.12	2.52	68	Marshall
Weeks (242, 109)	160	3.04	95	Marshall
Strand (93)	160	1.18	36	Marshall
Olson (10)	148.6	5.19	68	Marshall
Hellevang (143c)	147.25	2.71	50	Marshall
Wike (187, 362)	594.9	3.6	88.25	Roberts
Berwald et al (84, 93, 166)	560	1.88	64.4	Roberts
Loberg et al (11, 282, 286)	282.6	2.45	50	Roberts
Hamm-Elton (44, 114)	173.85	1.28	44.4	Roberts

PRIORITY LIST B

WPA	Acres	up/wet ratio	T-Storm score	County
Geise (200)	240	0.87	49.3	Clark
Evans-Kelly (314,502)	160.11	0.52	36	Clark
Graves (326)	147.99	1.38	50	Clark
Kadinger (24,a)	146.07	3.36	50	Clark
Poppen (324)	120	2.78	36	Clark
Kuecker (252)	80	2.59	36	Clark
Tulowetzke (31)	80	1.39	36	Clark
Kramer (11)	80	1.35	50	Clark
Struckmann-Trumm (30, 67)	261.38	0.94	36	Codington
David (124)	209.07	1.01	43.7	Codington
Geiger-Stevens-Page (89, 91, 92)	144.21	1.46	36.7	Codington
Owen-Mills (162, 165)	139.37	1.77	35.45	Codington
Swan (132)	137.92	1.4	36	Codington
Peterson (69)	80	2.35	50	Codington
Neal (127)	80	1.96	36	Codington
Dolney (40)	133.72	1.85	50	Day
Hanse-Rumpca (18, 139)	98.6	0.68	49.3	Day
Holden et al. (292, 293, 294)	81	1.59	36	Day
Wagner-Stianson (43, 57)	80	1.34	50	Day
McKane (288)	79.79	1.4	36	Day
East Storley (56 b)	75	1.67	50	Day
Case-Anderson et al (43, 44, 48)	227.13	0.75	68	Grant
Mogart-Street et al (53, 54, 142)	131.7	1.84	32.7	Grant
Antroinen-Broich (69, 172)	119.6	2.9	49.3	Grant
Miller-Schumacher (72, 75)	108.43	2.26	20	Grant
Garvey-Loehrer (62, 84)	104.84	3.5	15	Grant
Green (155)	87.3	7.78	81.5	Grant
Stink Slough (120a, 260)	400.43	0.74	50	Marshall
Keintz E. & W. (29)	174	1.78	30.5	Marshall
Gerber (221)	154	3.32	50	Marshall
Little Ruckdashel (11a)	143.2	3.33	68.54	Marshall
Guy C. East (257b)	120	5.49	68	Marshall
Fagerland E. (136)	85	0.94	50	Marshall
Hilleson-Sanderson (13, 30)	82.66	0.84	68	Marshall
Syverson (130, 246)	80.69	1.68	50	Marshall
Little Hinman (94)	80.21	2.96	59	Marshall
Silver Lake (257a)	80	3.88	50	Marshall
Bahr (12)	80	3.81	68	Marshall
Horseshoe Lake (171, 212, 214)	60.82	2.38	68	Marshall
Fonder-Okeson (134, 285)	401.6	0.69	25	Roberts
Danielson-Fladland (163, 173)	280	0.65	50	Roberts
Stowe (129)	160	0.83	50	Roberts
Kutter-Bredvik (113a, 148)	144.38	1.33	50	Roberts
Broz (211)	130.49	2.07	49.3	Roberts
Rolstad-Pearson (133, 352)	130.4	1.24	55.4	Roberts
Kutter et al (113, 136, 138)	125.8	0.93	50	Roberts
S.D-Eggen E. (2, 196)	120.8	5.46	51.8	Roberts
Navratil (130)	120	0.93	50	Roberts
Cameron (121)	119.04	1.04	30.5	Roberts
Knebel et al (147, 149, 150, 158)	117.2	0.83	68	Roberts
Minder-Dickinson (10, 132)	103.08	0.82	50	Roberts
Johnson (140)	80	3.4	36	Roberts

PRIORITY LIST C

WPA	Acres	up/wet ratio	T-Storm score	County
Froke-Waldow-Ness (372,373,374)	567.51	0.4	54.68	Clark
Saboe (476)	280.8	0.71	57.2	Clark
Smith (477,478)	189	0.64	48.6	Clark
Milburn-Foster (311,339)	177.37	0.38	36	Clark
Seefeldt (370)	170.83	1.06	50	Clark
Reinhart (10)	157.49	0.46	36.7	Clark
Ash-Moe (146,240)	147.69	0.44	50	Clark
Lee (315)	121.85	0.8	43	Clark
Storbeck (340)	103.85	0.61	36	Clark
Austin (312)	86.17	0.96	36	Clark
U.S. 1	80	0	36	Clark
Kannegieter, R. (18)	73.18	0.2	36	Clark
Wells (103)	60	1.32	36	Clark
Kannegieter, D. (92)	57.7	0.43	36	Clark
Evenson (328)	50	1.06	36	Clark
McLain (232)	46.62	0.56	36	Clark
Christopherson (241)	40	1.05	50	Clark
Hunt-Jennings (308,309)	38.79	0.41	36	Clark
Orthaus (119)	199.78	0.38	38.8	Codington
McClung (80a)	156.42	0.34	36	Codington
Briggs (130)	80	0.04	36	Codington
Elmore-Wasland (10, 234)	77.76	0.18	66.2	Codington
Halse-Grygiel (15, 38)	76.65	0.7	25	Codington
Burnstad (17)	48.95	0.42	25	Codington
Hansen (82)	45.35	3.3	41.6	Codington
Moorhouse (36)	42.58	0.28	15	Codington
Drake (160)	20	0	15	Codington
U.S. (1)	3.01	0	36	Codington
U.S. (1a)	0.98	0	68	Codington
Hozerland-Hamman (12,23,24)	205.71	0.26	41.6	Day
Lundeen (284)	149.94	0.93	49.5	Day
Dulitz (310)	149.67	0.61	50	Day
Akerson-Mattson (175, 338)	145.98	0.47	52.2	Day
Gruba-Teigen-Kwas. (243, 263,277)	133.87	0.35	50	Day
Hanson-Johnson (11, 20)	124	0.59	36	Day
Cramer (298)	109.47	0.68	36	Day
Gonsoir (132)	89.76	0.51	50	Day
Schmig (176)	82.46	0.43	50	Day
Fishbeck (44)	80	0.73	50	Day
Thompson (282)	80	0.02	50	Day
U.S. (1d)	80	0.02	50	Day
Denholm-Nelson (10, 193)	79.4	0.45	50	Day
Opitz (342)	70.8	0.8	36	Day
Schmit (194)	64.03	0.59	36	Day
Hilt (17)	62.12	0.55	50	Day
White-Stavig (170, 186)	44.85	0.35	43	Day
Eidahl (68)	44.84	0.88	50	Day
Bristol Grazing (197)	42.8	0.46	50	Day
Hawkinson (16)	40.94	1.79	36	Day
U.S. (1b)	40	0.32	50	Day
U.S. (1c)	40	0.23	68	Day
Wika (428)	40	0.16	36	Day
Nicolay (58)	40	0	31.6	Day
Bailly (45)	37.52	0.89	28.9	Day
Hubsch (229)	31.67	0.49	50	Day
Peterson (207)	27.69	0.38	36	Day
H. Hanson (146)	13.75	0.27	68	Day
U.S. (Antelope Lake) (1)	8.75	0	50	Day
Larson et al (63, 67, 68)	126.9	0.55	36	Grant
Streich (20)	79.24	0.62	17	Grant
Jensen (83)	71.84	3.24	15	Grant
Anderson (65)	65	1.2	25	Grant
Loehrer (84a)	48.08	1.55	25	Grant
Skoog (86)	46.01	1.54	15	Grant
Nelson (38)	34.06	0.62	68	Grant
Keeney (55)	34	0.64	15	Grant
Pew (10)	22.5	1.78	15	Grant
N. Ottertail (214c)	79.81	0.06	43	Marshall
Likness (92)	47.06	0.19	50	Marshall

S. Ottertail (214b)	40	0.03	50	Marshall
Osterman (119)	38.7	0.54	95	Marshall
Little Hauck (120)	16.99	0.11	50	Marshall
U.S. (1)	16.89	7.04	50	Marshall
Eickman (175)	78.5	2.27	36	Roberts
Carl (269)	75.4	2.22	36	Roberts
Pearson, M. (120)	75.2	0.11	25.6	Roberts
Remund (80, 351)	69.14	0.84	29.4	Roberts
Kastner (165)	65.52	1.98	50	Roberts
Pederson (181)	56.5	1.68	50	Roberts
Arndt (141, 142)	49.57	1.83	50	Roberts
Harsted-Elton (61, 127)	46.66	0.91	68	Roberts
Gleason (164)	44	1.4	50	Roberts
Meyer (167)	40.5	1.63	50	Roberts
Eggen W. (196)	40.11	2.31	68	Roberts
Eneboe (33)	34.6	1.02	36	Roberts
Stavig (122)	31.4	1.39	25	Roberts

Appendix I. Ecosystem Planning for the Mainstem Missouri River (condensed for CCP)

ECOSYSTEM PLAN
MAINSTEM MISSOURI RIVER
NORTH DAKOTA, SOUTH DAKOTA AND EAST MONTANA

TABLE OF CONTENTS

Mainstem Missouri River Ecosystem

Ecosystem Planning for the Mainstem Missouri Watersheds, including the Dakotas and Northeastern Montana

Prairies, wetlands, rivers. The contrasts are obvious, but a common thread runs through them: these habitats and the fish and wildlife that depend on them have undergone substantial change in the 200 years since Lewis and Clark ventured up the Missouri. Wetlands and native prairies have been converted to agricultural crop production and cities and towns. The "mighty Missouri" and many other rivers and streams have been dammed. The habitats that remain are increasingly more important to the region's fish and wildlife populations.

The U.S. Fish & Wildlife Service (Service) has adopted an ecosystem approach to conservation to fulfill its trust responsibilities with greater efficiency and effectiveness. Through this holistic approach to resource conservation, the Service can accomplish its mission to "conserve, protect, and enhance the Nation's fish, wildlife, and plants and their habitats for the continuing benefit of the American people."

An ecosystem approach to fish and wildlife conservation means protecting or restoring functions, structure, and species composition of an ecosystem while providing for its sustainable socioeconomic use. Key to implementing this approach will be recognizing that partnerships are an essential part of a diverse management team to accomplish ecosystem health.

The Service has adopted watersheds as the basic building blocks for implementing ecosystem conservation. The ecosystem includes portions of the Missouri River and Hudson Bay watersheds and is called the Missouri River Mainstem Ecosystem.

The Mainstem Ecosystem Team's Plan identified needs and set short and long-term goals and quantifiable objectives. The Team, with input from current partners and field stations, identified four focus areas; wetlands, native prairies, the Missouri River, and riparian areas. Priorities are based on significance in the ecosystem, species diversity, risk/threat to the entire focus area, public benefits, international values and trust resources. Also considered was a feasibility ranking based on legal mandates, opportunity for partnership, likelihood of success, cost effectiveness for activities, and significance of public land/private reserves.

This document is a first step to the implementation of an ecosystem approach to fish and wildlife conservation and calls for conserving fish and wildlife by protecting and restoring natural ecosystems.

WETLANDS

The glacia-ted prairies on North and South Dakota and northeastern Montana cover approximately 60 million acres. Once a myriad of prairie pothole wetlands in a sea of native prairie, the area is now the "brea-d basket" of the country and intensively farmed. Drainage, largely for agricultural purposes, has reduced 7.2 million acres of wetlands by over 40 percent, to 3.9 million acres. Native prairie, mostly mid-grass, has been reduced by 75 percent to 14.9 million acres. Much of the remainder is overgrazed by livestock.

The area is rich in wildlife. Prairie potholes are the lifeblood for waterfowl and other migratory water birds. As an example of the importance of the prairie wetlands, ducks bande-d in North Dakota have been recovered in 46 states and 23 other countries. Grassland nesting, neo-tropical birds have declined faster than woodland neotropica-ls or prairie nesting ducks. Several endangered and threatened species and species of management concern, including the ferruginous hawk, black tern, and Baird's sparrow, breed in the prairie and wetland habitats of this focus area.

Agriculture is the dominant economic activity and force on prairie wet-lands and grasslands. No other activity in the focus area affects habitats and wildlife populations to the extent that agriculture does. Simi-larly, USDA and the various federal farm programs have more influence on natural resources and wild-life than the Fish and Wildlife Service, all the state wildlife agencies and all the conservation organizations combined.

The Fish and Wildlife Service has been involved in prairie and wetland resources since the early 1900s. The Service has sixty-nine National Wildlife Refuges (380,000 acres) and nineteen Wetland Management Districts in the focus area. Since 1961, the Service's Small Wetland Acquisition Program has acquired 448,000 acres in fee-title and 1.9 million acres in perpetual easement. Since the 1985 Food Security Act, the Service has been involved with the USDA, in almost all wetland conversions on private land. Similarly, Service activities through the U.S. Army Corps of Engineer's administration of the Section 10/404 programs and the Fish and Wildlife Service Coordination Act have been focused on wetland resources.

The Prairie Pothole Joint Venture, including these three states, is a priority area for the North American Waterfowl Management Plan. As a result of the Joint Venture, the Service, other federal agencies, the state wildlife agencies, and a number of private conservation organizations, such as Ducks Unlimited, The Nature Conservancy, National Audubon Society, and the North Dakota Natural Resources, have formed excellent partnerships.

WETLANDS AND WATERSHEDS FOCUS AREA

Visions : Diverse, wetland habitats and watersheds that provide an abundance and diversity of native flora and fauna in the ecosystem for the benefit of the American public.

Goal 1: Increase recognition of wetland values by the various publics (communities, conservation organizations, communication people, Congressional delegations and staff, and corporate entities) to develop a wetland advocacy.

Objective A: Over the next 3 years, de-velop and implement an information and outreach plan in North and South Dakota and northeastern Mon-tana. (Work with EVS Bran-ch)

Goal 2: Conserve, restore, and enhance wetlands and wetland habitats and functions for trust species and species of concern.

Objective A: As a minimum, annually protect 15,000 acres of wetlands through fee and easement over the next 10 years in the ecosystem.

Objective B: Assist partners and other agencies in protecting, creating, restoring, managing, and en-han-cing 10,000 acres of wetlands and associated uplands annually.

Goal 3: Protect the water supply and property interests of wetlands on Service lands and easements. (This goal will be further defined with the Water Rights Division)

Objective A: File for and secure water rights on eligible Service properties and easements over the next 10 years.

MISSOURI RIVER

Prior to the early 1900-s, the Missouri River was characterized by ever eroding banks, shifting side channels, heavily wooded islands, abundant bottoml-ands, and myriad sandbars. The "Big Muddy'-s" con-stantly changing nature supported one of North America's most diverse and extensive aquatic and riparian ecosystems. Today the Missouri River is vastly different from that "untamed" floodplain system of even 50 years ago. Originating in the Rocky Mountains of south-central Montana, the River flows 2,300 miles, traversing seven States and passing through seven mainstem dams built and maintained by the Federal Government. Over 900 miles (nearly 60 percent) of the former upper River passing through Montana, North Dakota, South Dakota and Nebraska, now lie under permanent multi-purpose reservoirs. Construction and management of these dams transformed a complex natural riverine system and caused profound physical and natural changes to the River.

As the Missouri River changed, so did the wildlife communities that depended so com-pletely upon it. Impoundments, channelization, and subsequent control of water discharges have significantly reduced population levels and reproductive success of some nature species. Currently, eight fish species, 15 birds, six mammals, four reptiles, six insects, four mollusks, and seven plants indigenous to the system are listed as either threatened or endangered or are under status review for possible listing. One of the Missouri River fauna groups most severely impacted by the chang-es was the endemic fish populations. Large river species, like the sturgeon and paddlefish, have experienced serious population declines and loss of reproduction as a result of the changes to the System.

Although the Missouri River ecosystem can never be returned to its predevelopm-ent state, some of the ongoing destructive processes can be modified and the overall condition of the ecosystem improved. Actions can be taken toward recovery of the river's biological integrity, while retaining developmental purposes such as flood control, recreation and water supply. A holistic plan of action involving such diverse entities as the States, Tribes, Federal Agencies, and private interests will be required to accomplish the needed rejuvenation of the Missouri River. This plan must involve a coordinated, system-based approach which recognizes the needs of the Basin's fish and wildlife re-sources, and the public benefits they impart, in addition to facilitating developmental needs and values.

MISSOURI RIVER FOCUS AREA

Visions: A healthy Missouri River capable of self-sustaining fish and wildlife resources.

Goal 1:   Reestablish some semblance of the natural form and function of the Missouri River and prevent further degradation for priority riverine sections.

Objective A: Implement provisions of the Services Reasonable and Prudent Alternative described in the Missouri River Biological Opinion(November 30,2000).

1. Achieve a more ecologically beneficial hydro graph below Ft. Peck, Garrison, Ft. Randall, and Gavins Point Dams by working with COE, States, and other stakeholders by 2003.
2. Work with the COE, States, and stakeholders to achieve compatible ecologically beneficial water quality parameters including temperature, sediment transport, and turbidity by 2003.
3. Increase functional habitat base in prioritized riverine sections through restorations, creations, and modification/enhancement where opportunities allow. Attempt one major project per year beginning in 2001.

Objective B: Work with local zoning authorities and regulators to develop and implement policies that discourage floodplain development and bank stabilization to maintain/restore river functions by 2003.

Objective C: Continue an environmental contaminants presence on the Missouri River that monitors conditions, identifies issues and problem areas, and develops strategies for rehabilitation.

Objective D: Identify strategies and implement partnerships that maintain and restore riparian values, with emphasis on cottonwood regeneration.

Objective E: Develop and implement a conservation strategy that protects riparian values at the confluence of the Missouri and Yellowstone Rivers (2004).

Goal 2:   Conserve endangered and threatened species and species of special concern in riverine and impounded reaches, consistent with other Service objectives.

Objective A: Augment current pallid sturgeon populations in: 1) the Missouri River above Ft. Peck Reservoir, 2) the Missouri and Yellowstone Rivers above Lake Sakakawea, and 3) below Gavins Point Dam through hatchery production to develop a genetically sound natural population structure by 2011.

Objective B: Achieve a 3-year running average fledged success rate of 0.70 for 325 pairs of least terns, and 1.13 for 350 pairs of piping plovers on the Missouri River system by 2011.

Objective C: Develop management strategies plans for the sicklefin chub and the sturgeon chub by 2002, and seek funding and implementation of plans by 2004 in order to prevent declines in their population status.

Objective D: Establish priority and complete status reviews for species of special concern, such as the blue sucker, flathead chub, western silvery and plains minnows, initiating one species per year beginning in 2002.

Objective E: Monitor threats and develop strategies to eliminate or minimize affects of invasive species on native aquatic resources.

Objective F: Work with partners and the Upper Missouri/Yellowstone Team to relieve fish passage barriers on the Yellowstone River (2005).

Goal 3:   Strive for a fully informed public on Missouri River natural resource issues and activities.

Objective A: Promote restoration of river functions and values through proactive outreach.

Objective B: Seek support and partnerships for River activities through proactive outreach.

Goal 4:   Fulfill commitments for mitigation of fishery resources brought about by construction of the mainstem dams.

Objective A: Through hatcheries, management, and conservation, support State fisheries objectives for the Missouri River and its impoundments consistent with other Service objectives.

NATIVE PRAIRIE GRASSLANDS

Prairie habitats in the Mainstem Mis-souri ecosystem consist of tall grass, mid-grass, and short grass prai-ries from the eastern Dakotas to the west. Although the plant and wildlife species differ across the gradation from tall to short grass, the threats and issues remain the same; conversion of prairie to other uses. Habitat losses have been the most severe in the tall grass, and least in the western reaches of the Dakotas and northeastern Montana.

The tallgrass prairie once spanned millions of acres along the eastern border of North and South Dakota. The tallgrass prairie is characterized by big bluestem, switch grass, Indian grass, and prairie dropseed. In North Dakota this is found main-ly in the Agas-siz Lake plain, but transitionally can be found along the State's east-ern bor-der in a strip 2-3 counties wide. Similarly in South Dakota the zone follows the eastern border at a sim-ilar width broadening to the Missouri River at the south-ern end of the State. Most of the tallgra-ss habitat has been con-verted to agriculture. The remaining tall gra-ss prai-rie sites are found in small frag-mented parcels scattered through-out and are crucial to main-taining and restoring the ecosystem. These sites are threatened by con-version to cropland; invasion by exo-tics, noxious weeds, and woody plant-s; pesticides; and heavy grazing pressure.

The remaining tallgrass prairie sites support a wide assemblage of plant and animal species including many Federal and State rare species. Sites in North Dakota have the largest population of the western prairie fringed orchid, a federally threatened plant found in lowland swales within the tallgra-ss community. Other species of concern in-clude the regal fritillary, Dakota skip-per and the powesheik skipper, all butterflies which are species of management concern. Eighteen state classified rare plants occur in tallgrass prairie of North Dakota. The tallgrass prai-rie also provides primary and secondary breeding habitat for neotropic-al migrants in decline such as the upland plover, bobolink, common yellowthroat, grasshopper sparrow, clay-colored sparrow, Baird's sparrow, and loggerhead shrike. Long-term survival of these small, isolated prairies depends on establishing prairie networks and connecting these prairies and nearby habitats to ward off extinction, and integrating prairies with their surrounding to reduce harm from improper management on surrounding lands.

The native prairie west of the tallgrass area in the two Dakotas consists primarily of mixed grass prairie with some shortgrass prairie in the far western portion of the two Dakotas.

In the east river portions of the Dakotas, over half the historic native prairie has been converted to cropland, tame hayland, or other uses. Statistics from the Natural Resources Conservation Service's (NRCS) NRI data indicate the east river North Dakota has lost about 403,000 acres of native range between 1982 and 1997. Similar statistics for South Dakota show a 519,000 acre loss of native range in east river South Dakota. Much of the remaining native prairie in private ownership is overused for livestock. Native grasslands in public ownership are often under-managed and idled for too long without prescribed treatments, and are invaded by introduced and exotic plant species. Nevertheless these native east river prairies are important as cover for a wide variety of migratory birds, resident wildlife species, and species of management concern such as the Dakota skipper, Baird's sparrow, upland plover, and the ferruginous hawk. In addition, native prairie grasslands protect the watersheds for prairie wetlands and streams and rivers in the east river country. Wetlands located in grasslands managed for livestock are more secure from drainage than those located in cropland or more intensive agricultural situations.

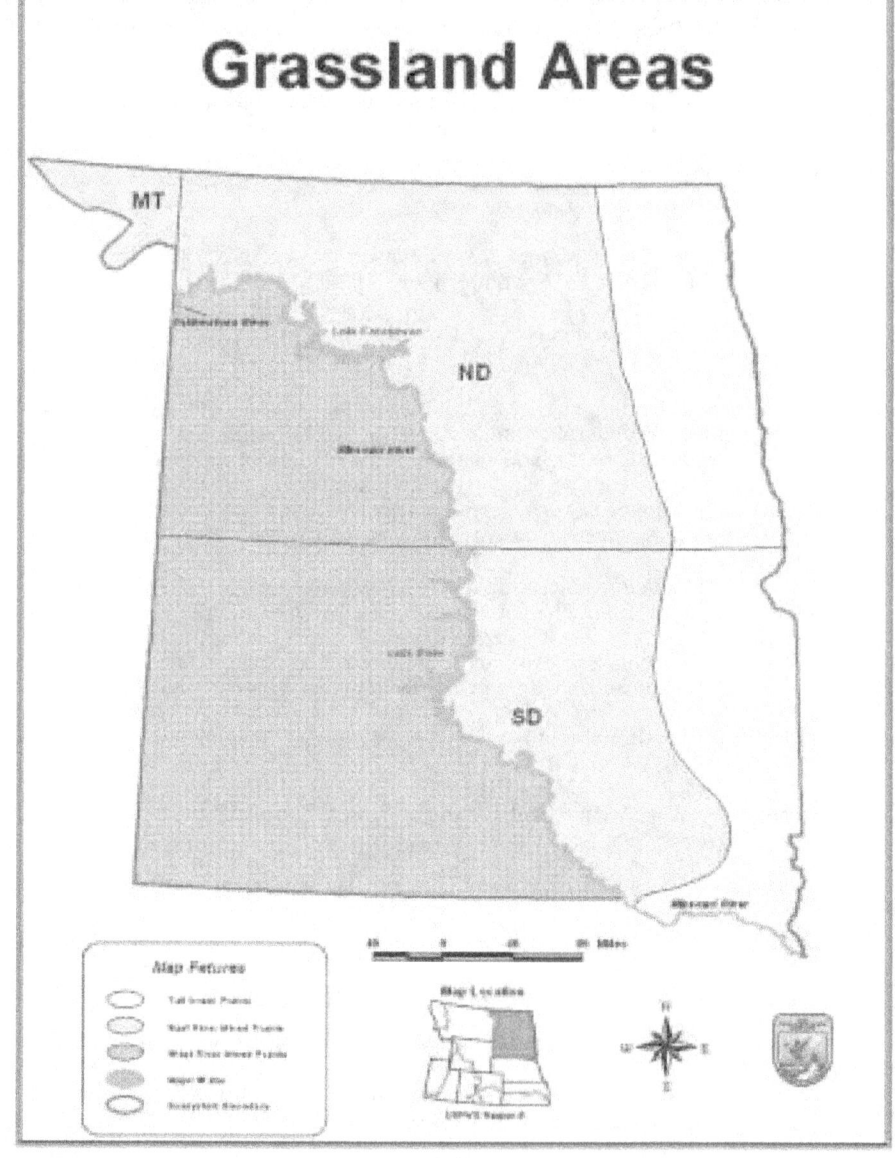

The west river area of North and South Dakota, located west of the Missouri River has lost approximately 40 percent (60 percent for North Dakota and 30 percent for South Dakota) of the original 34 million acres of native prairie due to agricultural conversion. These losses are compounded by overgrazing on much of the remaining acres. Some of the remaining prairie is in public ownership managed by several federal agencies, primarily the U.S. Forest Service with about 1.6 million acres of National Grasslands. Another 4.5 million acres in South Dakota and 1.5 million acres in North Dakota are under tribal jurisdiction. NRCS NRI data show a 480,000 acre native prairie loss in west river South Dakota and a 184,000 acre loss in North Dakota during the 1982-1997 period. The continual decline of prairie has re-sulted in habitat fragmentation of the native prairie in the west river. Grassland conversion and overuse of the grasslands results in a loss of natural habitat diversity through the decline in vegetative species and the establishment of introduced and exotic plants. West River native prairies support a wide variety of migratory birds including high numbers of waterfowl in certain areas, endangered and threatened species and species of management concern. A major species found west river is the black-tailed prairie dog and its colonies which provide habitat for over 130 vertebrate species. Past and continued reduction of black-tailed prairie dogs from the landscape jeopardizes a number of species, most notably the black-footed ferret, swift fox, and burrowing owl. Also included in the west river area of both states are 2 million acres of "badlands", two areas of highly eroded, rugged topography. The South Dakota badlands are mostly under the management of the National Park Service in Badlands National Park; in North Dakota the badlands are mostly within the jurisdiction of the U.S. Forest Service.

Visions: Protect, restore and maintain ecosystem native prairie and other grasslands to ensure its diversity and abundance of indigenous flora and fauna.

Goal 1: Prevent degradation and conversion of native prairie grassland.

Objective A: Locate, categorize, evaluate and map native prairie within the ecosystem for baseline information by 2003.

Objective B: Protect native prairie by FWS easement on a minimum of 100,000 acres per year for the next 10 years.

Objective C: By the year 2003, develop and implement informational programs to promote awareness and advocacy for native prairie.

Objective D: Develop partnerships to protect 1,000,000 acres of native prairie by 2010.

Objective E: Develop partnerships to reduce the extent and curtail the impact of invasive species in native prairie by 2010.

Objective F: Strive to work with partners to reduce fragmentation effects to flora and fauna in native prairie communities.

Objective G: Identify contaminant issues affecting native prairie and the adverse impact each may be on native prairie and associated wildlife species.

Objective H: Develop a plan, on how to prevent and/or reduce further contaminants from entering native prairie.

Goal 2: Maintain and establish networks of native prairie and planted grasslands on public and private lands.

Objective A: Promote and implement prescribed burning and rotational grazing on a minimum of 20 percent of private lands per year to enhance and maintain healthy native prairie.

Objective B: By the year 2003, develop informational materials on the importance of proper grazing management of native prairie.

Objective C: By the year 2002 identify the key areas in the ecosystem to restore perennial grasslands, maintain and/or increase planted grassland with an emphasis on native species restoration.

Objective D: Strive to treat a minimum of 20 percent of FWS administered grasslands annually using prescribed fire, prescribed grazing, invasive species control or other recognized man-agement practice.

Goal 3: Protect, restore and enhance habitat for trust species and species of special concern.

Objective A: Identify declining grassland species of wildlife by the year 2003.

Objective B: Develop information programs on why grassland species in decline are important, approaches to be taken to reverse decline, and the public's role in prairie conservation.

Objective C: Develop statewide partnerships to get people involved in species management.

Objective D: Develop criteria and identify the most biologically significant grasslands by 2003.

Objective E: Over the next 10 years, develop partnerships to enhance and man-age native prairie including invasion by nonnative species.

Objective F: Develop management strategies to enhance species of concern on priority grasslands.

RIPARIAN AREAS

Riparian areas make up a very small portion of the habitat in the Ecosystem. However, riparian and riverine wetland habitats are very important to fish and wildlife resources including migratory birds, threatened and endangered species, native fish, rare and declining fisheries, amphibians and many mammals. Many vertebrates including species of nongame and neotrop-ical migratory birds, are dependent on riparian and adjacent aquatic zones for reproduction or for foraging during reproduction. Riparian habitats provide for much of the biodiversity in the ecosystem. Many of the species currently occurring in the ecosystem would be eliminated without healthy riparian habitats.

Riparian habitats are impor-tant even to the species that main-ly occur in the adjacent upland areas. Many rare and declining neotropic-al prairie grassland species need to nest a short distance from water, and will use riparian areas during juvenile dispersal and as critical sites of migratory stopovers. Many wildlife species use these zones as migratory corridors. Riparian habitats are also important for stabilizing riverbanks, reducing sedimentation, providing woody debris, and organic material for invertebrates, thus enhancing fish habitat. Many resident wildlife species use riparian areas for winter survival. These species leave the upland areas, using the riparian areas for food and cover during the winter.

National Wildlife Refuges occur along the Missouri, Souris, James, Des Lacs, and Red River and their tributaries. These refuges include sites of internationally significant Prairie Pothole Joint Venture projects critical to success of the North American Waterfowl Management Plan. Riparian wetlands in the Missouri River system are nursery areas for forage fish vital to survival of the Federally endangered pallid sturgeon and least tern, and a variety of candidate species.

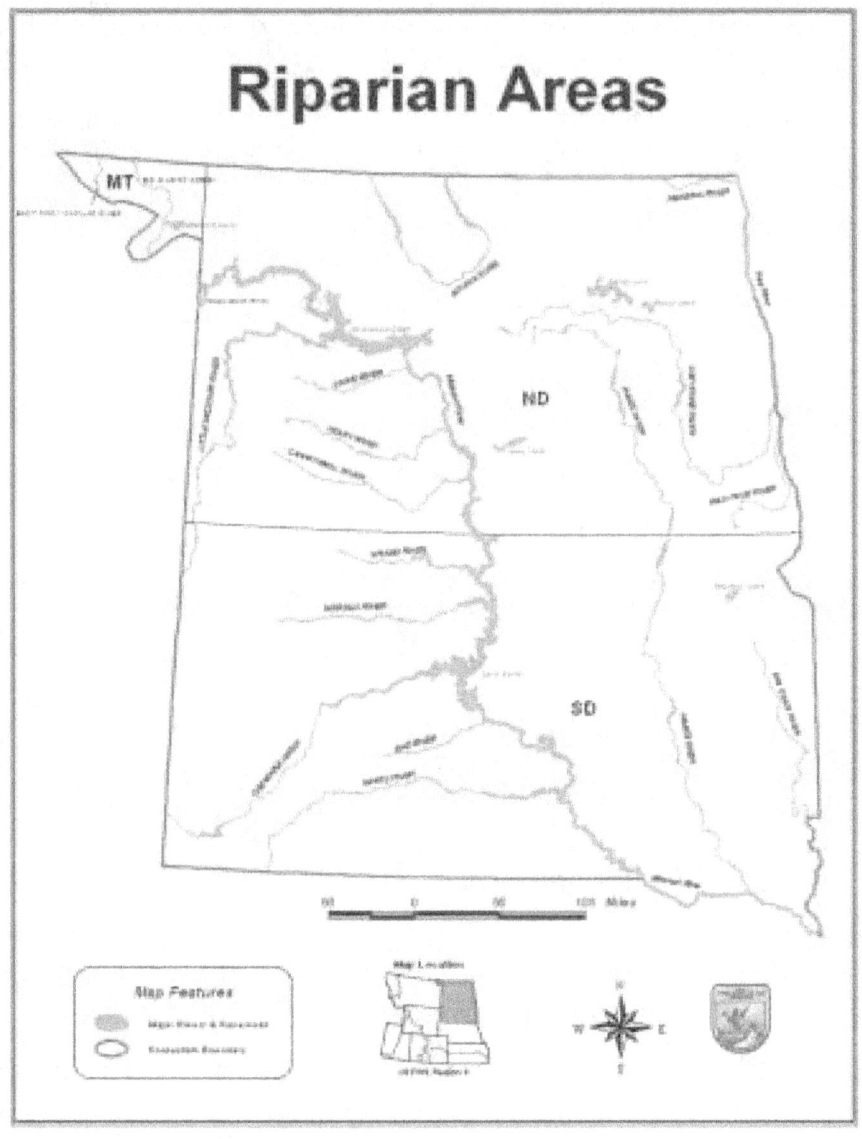

Opportunities for partnerships will increase as people realize that pro-active, ecosystem-based management can head off listing of endangered species in this wildlife-rich area that contains food, energy, and water supplies of global importance.

RIPARIAN FOCUS AREA

<u>Visions</u>: Healthy riparian and floodplain ecosystems that provide an abundance and diversity of indigenous flora and fauna.

<u>Goal 1</u>: Reduce the conversion of riparian habitats and maintain, restore or enhance existing riparian habitats, quality and func-tions on priority rivers and trib-utaries.

Objective A: Inventory and determine the quality of riparian hab-itats and associated wildlife populations within the ecosystem by 2004 to provide baseline informa-tion.

Objective B: Implement an informational program in the ecosystem by 2004 to promote a public appreciation and understanding of the benefits and the threats to riparian habitats.

Objective C: Support and assist in locating and control of invasive species in the ecosystem by 2006 to maintain or improve the quality of the riparian habitat and protect National Wildlife Refuges and other important habitats.

Objective D: Use existing programs and opportunities in the ecosystem by 2009 to improve critical riparian habitats.

<u>Goal 2</u>: Conserve and recover threatened and endangered species and species of management concern.

Objective A: Inventory threatened and endangered species and species of concern along riparian corridors in the ecosystem by 2004 to provide baseline information.

Objective B: Develop and implement strategies for conserving and recovering threatened and endangered species and species of concern along riparian habitats in the ecosystem by 2004 and preclude the need to list any further species.

<u>Goal 3</u>: Conserve, restore, and create habitat resources in watersheds to enhance the quality and quantity of water flowing into rivers and streams.

Objective A: Use existing oversight, coordination and technical assistance by 2006 to promote sound management on critical watersheds in the ecosystem.

Objective B: Use existing programs and opportunities in the ecosystem by 2006 to conserve, enhance or restore grasslands and wetlands to provide quality water runoff.

Appendix A. Mainstem Missouri Ecosystem Decision Matrix Criteria

1) Threatened and endangered species. 15 Points

The intent of this criteria is to give more weight to proposals demonstrating a direct benefit to the greatest number of imperiled species, those species that are in greatest need of assistance, and proposals that move the species towards recovery.

Species Status

Endangered	5 points *	# of endangered species benefitted =
Threatened	3 points *	# of threatened species benefitted =
Proposed	2 points *	# of proposed species benefitted =
Species of Mgt. Concern: 1 point *		# of candidate species =

2) Migratory Birds.   15 Points Maximum

Provides habitat for raptors:	3 points
Provides habitat for passerines:	3 points
Provides habitat for ducks, geese, and swans:	3 points
Provides habitat for shorebirds and other wetland obligate species:	3 points
Provides habitat for 3 or more of the migratory bird groups above:	3 points

3) Large, Intact Landscapes.   15 Points Maximum

> 5000 acres:	5 points
1000 - 5000 acres:	1 point
< 1000 acres:	3 points

Land adjoining or expanding upon areas already protected (i.e. subject to state and/or federal resource):   3 points

Disturbance/Restoration Potential

Little to no disturbance (pristine):	4 points
Slight disturbance (easily restored):	3 points
Moderate disturbance (moderate restoration required:	2 points
Significant restoration required:	1 point
Heavily disturbed (cannot be restored)	0 points
Lands that create corridors linking priority habitats	3 points

4) Fisheries. 15 Points Maximum

High quality habitat present:	5 points
Habitat capable of being restored:	4 points
Presence of indigenous species:	3 points
Absence of nonnative or invasive species:	3 points

5) Degree and Immediacy of Threats. 15 Points Maximum

This criteria measures the immediacy as well as the potential degree and extent of threats facing a particular resource.

Degree of Threat:		Immediacy of Threat:	
High degree of	8 points	Immediate and imminent action pending:	7 points
Medium degree	5 points	Moderate chance of impending action:	4 points
Low degree of	2 points	Slight chance of impending action:	1 point

6) Good Opportunities. 10 Points Maximum

Ten or more partners:	Yes / No
Identified as a "Focus Area" by NGO or other agency:	Yes / No
At least a 3:1 non-FWS match available:	Yes / No
Watershed group in place:	Yes / No
Defined and measurable objectives:	Yes / No
Multiple native species benefits:	Yes / No
Excellent (6 of 6 criteria met):	10 points
Very Good (5 of 6):	7 points
Good (4 of 6):	5 points
Fair (3 of 6):	3 points
Poor (2 or less):	1 point

7) Likelihood of Achieving Objective(s) as Defined in Mainstream Missouri Plan 10 Points Maximum

Will meet most objective(s):	10 points
Will meet most objective(s):	7 points
Will meet some objective(s):	4 points
Does not meet objective(s):	0 points

8) Cost/Benefits 5 Points Maximum

(Units other than area may require different multipliers.)

Less that $300 per acre:	5 points
$300-$700 per acre:	3 points
Greater than $700 per acre:	1 point

GRAND TOTAL (100 Points Maximum) =

GRASSLAND EASEMENT EVALUATION WORKSHEET

NAME:	COUNTY:
ADDRESS:	LEGAL DESCRIPTION:
TELEPHONE:	
TRACT SIZE:	WETLAND MANAGEMENT DISTRICT:

Ranking Factors

		(5)	(4)	(3)	(2)	(1)	Factor		Score
1.	Grassland Easement Location	on wetland easement	adjacent to fee title or wet. ease.	Adjacent to public water	within 1 mile of fee or ease.	--		x3	
2.	Grassland Quality (% of total area)	(Choose the line with the highest point value)							
	Native Prairie	>75	50-74	25-49	0-24	—		x3	
	Tame Grasses/DNC	---	---	50-100	25-49	<25		x2	
	Tame Grasses/Interior	---	---	---	50-100	<50		x1	
	Cropland/Native	---	—	50-100	25-49	<25		x1	
	Cropland/DNC	—	---	—	50-100	<50		x1	
	Cropland/Interior	← disqualified for easement →							
3.	Distance from perpetually protected brood water or, "thunderstorm Map" siting	on the tract (Red/Yellow) 100 - 96%	within 0.5 miles 81 - 95%	0.5 - 1.0 miles 61 - 80%	— 41 - 60%	— 21 - 40%		x3	
4.	Number of Wetland Basins/Square Mile or, "Thunderstorm Map" siting	50+ (Red/Yellow) 100 - 96%	30 -49 81 - 95%	15 - 29 61 - 80%	5 - 14 41 - 60%	1 - 4 21 - 40%		x3	
5.	Tract Size (acres)	640+	480 - 639	320 - 479	240 - 319	160 - 239		x3	
6.	Soil Capability	85 - 100% of upland is highly erodible soil or Capability Class IV+	70 - 84%	50 - 69%	20 - 49%	<20%		x2	
7.	Special Features (Bonus Points - One Point each)								
	a. Low brush, woody cover, riparian habitat with benefits to waterfowl or non-game migratory birds							x1	
	b. Habitat with benefits to endangered species							x1	
	c. Easement will help control saline seeps, existing contaminant problems, etc.							x1	
	d. Landowner simultaneously signs grassland management agreement or easement is part of a partnership project.							x3	
	e. Other (specify)							x1	
						Total Score:			
						Threshold Score:			

Evaluator:	Recommended:
Date:	Not Recommended:
Supervisor:	

Appendix K. Existing Partnerships

The following organizations, agencies and individuals have been instrumental in helping us to meet current objectives for protecting or restoring habitat or improving and providing public use, education or interpretation.

Federal Emergency Management Agency
U.S. Department of Agriculture
    Natural Resource Conservation Service
    Farm Service Agency
    APHIS
Sisseton-Wahpeton Sioux Tribe
South Dakota Game, Fish and Parks
South Dakota Conservation Commission
Soil and Water Conservation Districts: Grant, Day, Roberts, Marshall, Clark, Codington
Minnesota Area III Conservation Districts
Friends of Big Stone Lake
Ducks Unlimited, Inc.
Pheasants Forever
The Nature Conservancy
Glacial Lakes Outdoor School
Boy and Girl Scouts of America
North American Wetlands Conservation Council
Aberdeen Development corporation
East Dakota Water Development District
Watershed groups for Lake Farley, Big Stone Lake, Lake Kampeska, Lake Traverse
SD Chapter of The Wildlife Society
American Fisheries Society - Dakota Chapter
National Audubon Society
HT Enterprises, Inc.
SD Army National Guard
Izaak Walton League of America - Kampeska Chapter
Scheels All Sports
Dave Genz and The Ice Team
Lindy Little Joe, Inc.
Berkely
Hundreds of private landowners
Beth Ullenburg - Outdoor Recreation Planner, Sand Lake NWR
Bob Losco - Conservation Officer, South Dakota Game, Fish and Parks
Kari Sorenson - NE-SO-DAK
Numerous other individuals who have helped over the years with various programs or projects

Appendix L. Compatibility Determinations

The following activities were previously covered under compatibility determinations evaluated in 1994 to comply with a court order. During the process of the Comprehensive Conservation Plan these activities have been reevaluated and determined to comply with the compatibility standards.

- Upland Management - Waubay NWR Complex
- Deer Hunting - Waubay NWR
- Waterfowl, Upland Game and Deer Hunting - Waubay WMD
- Sport Fishing - Waubay WMD
- Trapping of Furbearers - Waubay WMD
- Education and Interpretation - Waubay NWR
- Cross Country Skiing - Waubay NWR
- Picnicking - Waubay NWR

An Environmental assessment was completed for Management of Upland Habitat on Waubay NWR and Waubay WMD. It was found to have no significant impact.

Copies of these compatibility determinations and Environmental Assessment are located at the Waubay NWR Complex Headquarters.

As in the past, prior to new activities occurring or permitted in the Complex a compatibility determination and NEPA documentation is completed and concurrence is obtained by the Regional Office.

When new activities or actions are proposed and found to have significant impacts affecting the quality of the human environment or there is disagreements on the impacts, an Environmental Assessment or Environmental Impact Statement is required and includes public input on the decision process.

Compatibility Overview

Compatibility is a tool refuge managers use to ensure that recreation and other uses do not interfere with wildlife conservation - the primary focus of refuges. For purposes of this document, uses are any recreational, economic/commercial, pest/predator control, or other use of the refuge by the public or a non-Service entity. Compatibility is not new to the Refuge System and dates back to 1918, as a concept. As policy, it has been used since 1962. The Refuge Recreation Act of 1962 (Recreation Act) directed the Secretary of Interior to allow only those public uses of refuge lands that were "compatible with the primary purposes for which the area was established." This law also required that adequate funds be available for administration and protection of refuges before opening them to any public uses. Legally, refuges are closed to all public uses until officially opened through a compatibility determination.

The National Wildlife Refuge System Administration Act of 1966 set a compatibility standard which refuge managers used until new compatibility regulations, required by the National Wildlife Refuge System Improvement Act of 1997 (Refuge System Improvement Act), were adopted. The Refuge System Improvement Act maintains a compatibility standard but provides more detail regarding the standard and the process, and requires the process be promulgated in regulations. It also requires that a use must be compatible with both the mission of the System <u>and</u> the purposes of the individual refuge, which helps to ensure consistency in application across the System. The Act also requires that the public have an opportunity to comment on use evaluations. This Act stipulates that the needs of wildlife must come first and defines a compatible use as a use that ". . . in the sound professional judgement of the Director, will not materially interfere with or detract from the fulfillment of the mission of the [NWRS] or the purposes of the refuge." Sound professional judgement is defined as ". . . a finding, determination, or decision, that is consistent with principles of sound fish and wildlife management and administration, available science and resources. . . ." Compatibility for priority wildlife-dependent uses may depend on the level or extent of a use.

In 1978, the compatibility standard was tested in court when recreational uses at Ruby Lake NWR (water skiing and motor boating) were found to be in violation of the Refuge Recreation Act. The court determined that compatibility is a biological standard and cannot be used to balance or weigh economic, political, or recreational interests against the primary purpose of the refuge. This ruling stated that the existence of noncompatible uses on a refuge in the past has no bearing on the compatibility of present uses. In their summary of this case, Coggins et al. (1987) conclude "neither poor administration of the Refuge in the past nor prior interferences with its primary purpose, nor past recreational, nor deterioration of its wildlife resources since establishment, nor administrative custom or tradition alters the statutory standard."

The Service recognizes that compatibility determinations are complex. For this reason Refuge Managers are required to consider "principles of sound fish and wildlife management" and "available science" in making these determinations. Evaluations of the existing uses on Waubay Complex are based on the professional judgement of refuge personnel including observations of refuge uses and reviews of appropriate scientific literature.

The compatibility determinations that follow are consistent with the Compatibility Policy and Regulations published in the Federal Register (FR 62484, FR 62458).

1. Use:
2. Refuge Name:
3. Establishing and Acquisition Authorities:
4. Refuge Purposes:
5. NWRS Mission:
6. Description of Use:
7. Availability of Resources:
8. Anticipated Impacts of the Use:
9. Public Review and Comment:
10. Determination:
11. Stipulations Necessary to Ensure Compatibility:
12. Justification:

Items 2 through 5 are listed once in the beginning of this document. Items 1 and 6 through 12 will be listed for each determination.

Compatibility determinations for the following uses are included within this appendix:

- Environmental Education and Interpretation
- Wildlife Observation & Wildlife Photography
- Fishing
- Hunting
- Trapping
- Farming, Grazing and Haying
- Research

Compatibility Determinations

Refuge Name:
Waubay National Wildlife Refuge Complex (Complex)

Establishing and Acquisition Authority(ies):
Waubay National Wildlife Refuge:
    Established on December 10, 1935

Waubay Wetland Management District:
    Established on August 1, 1958

Waubay National Wildlife Refuge located in Day County, South Dakota was established by Executive Order 7245 "as a refuge and breeding ground for migratory birds and other wildlife."

Waubay Wetland Management District is part of the Small Wetland Acquisition Program (SWAP) started in the 1950s to save wetlands from various threats, particularly draining. The passage of Public Law 85-585 on August 1, 1958, amended the Migratory Bird Hunting and Conservation Stamp Act (Duck Stamp Act) of 1934, allowing for the acquisition of "Waterfowl Production Areas" and "Easements for Waterfowl Management Rights" (easement). The Wetland Loan Act (P.L. 87-383) was passed on October 4, 1961 and allowed for the advancement of the funds against future revenues from Duck Stamp sales. As a result, Wetland Management Districts (WMD) were created in 1962.

Refuge Complex Purpose(s):
- For lands acquired under Executive Order 7245, dated Dec 10, 1935, the purpose of the acquisition is ". . . as a refuge and breeding ground for migratory birds and other wildlife . . . ."
- For WMD lands acquired under Public Law 85-585, dated August 1, 1958, the purpose of the acquisition is to assure the continued availability of habitat capable of supporting migratory bird populations at desired levels.
- For lands acquired under the Migratory Bird Hunting and Conservation Stamp Tax, 16 U.S.C. 718, as amended, for the purpose: ". . . as Waterfowl Production Areas" subject to . . . all of the provisions of such Act [Migratory Bird Conservation Act] . . . except the inviolate sanctuary provisions . . . 11 16 U.S.C. S 718 (Migratory Bird Hunting and Conservation Stamp Act).

National Wildlife Refuge System Mission:
The National Wildlife Refuge System mission is to administer a national network of lands and waters for the conservation, management and, where appropriate, restoration of the fish, wildlife and plant resources and their habitats within the United States for the benefit of present and future generations of Americans.

Use: Environmental Education and Interpretation

Description of Use:

Environmental education consists of activities conducted by Complex staff, volunteers, NeSoDak staff (a Service Partner) and teachers. Interpretation occurs in less formal activities with Complex staff and volunteers or through exhibits, educational trunks, signs, and brochures. Currently, environmental education and interpretation activities are conducted at the Complex office/visitor center. Programs and activities are also held at various locations on the Complex Headquarters Island and on Waterfowl Production Areas (WPA's) throughout the Wetland Management District (District). Additional programs are conducted at schools and other locations as personnel are available. The CCP calls for establishing an environmental education center located near the Complex office. This facility will permit school groups to maximize their time at the Complex Headquarters in environmental education activities during a limited school day. The current outdoor education site is equipped with facilities for school groups to have lunch while participating in all day events. The remainder of the Refuge serves as a sanctuary for wildlife. Cross country skiing and snowshoeing on established hiking trails will be allowed during winter months. These uses occur year-round with peak use in the spring and fall for environmental education.

The CCP proposes to continue with the above uses and add the following to improve environmental education and interpretation opportunities and access for all visitors.

- Hire an Outdoor Recreation Planner
- Construct a new Education Center
- Construct a boardwalk and observation deck
- Update and improve Complex Signs
- Construct new entrance kiosk and update existing kiosk panels
- Establish a Coteau Birding Trail with sites located on the Refuge and WPA's
- Update existing brochures to new Service standards
- Pave headquarter/visitor center and trail head parking lots with asphalt or concrete

Availability of Resources:

Currently all above activities are conducted using available Complex staff. Funding is adequate to continue with our current outreach activities. Additional funds will be required to provide additional programs and activities as outlined in the CCP.

Anticipated Impacts of Use:

Anticipated impacts from environmental education and interpretation are minor damage to vegetation, littering, possible conflict with other users, and increased maintenance activity. Minor disturbances to wildlife were considered during planning. Location and time limitations placed on environmental education and interpretation activities assure that this activity has only minor impacts on wildlife and does not detract from the primary purposes of the Refuge.

Public Review and Comment:

This Compatibility Determination was distributed for public review and comment as an appendix to the draft Comprehensive Conservation Plan and Environmental Assessment for Waubay National Wildlife Refuge Complex.

Determination (check one below):

_____Use is Not Compatible

___X___ Use is Compatible With the Following Stipulations

Stipulations Necessary to Ensure Compatibility:

Environmental education and interpretation will only occur in designated areas or under the guidance of a Complex staff member, volunteer, or trained teacher to assure minimal disturbance to wildlife, minimal vegetation damage, and minimal conflict between user groups. Environmental education and interpretation activities will be reviewed annually to ensure this compatibility determination still applies.

Justification:

Based upon biological impacts described in the CCP and Environmental Assessment, it is determined that environmental education and interpretation within the Waubay National Wildlife Refuge Complex will not materially interfere with or detract from the purposes for which this Complex was established.

Secondly, environmental education and interpretation are priority public uses listed in the National Wildlife Refuge System Improvement Act. By facilitating environmental education on the Complex, we will increase knowledge and appreciation of fish, wildlife and their habitats among program participants, which will lead to increased public stewardship of wildlife and their habitats at the Complex and elsewhere. Increased public stewardship will support and complement the Service's actions in achieving the Complex's purposes and the mission of the National Wildlife Refuge System.

Mandatory 10- or 15-year Re-evaluation Date: 2017

Use: Wildlife Observation and Wildlife Photography

Description of Use:
Currently, wildlife observation and wildlife photography occurs along the Complex Headquarters entrance road, walking trails and the observation tower at the Complex Headquarters. Wildlife observation and wildlife photography also take place throughout the Wetland Management District, mostly on Waterfowl Production Areas. These activities occur throughout the year but main interest is during the spring and fall migrations. Access for wildlife observation and wildlife photography is gained through hiking, bicycling, and by automobile. Automobile and bicycling are only allowed on the entrance road and public roads located along and through WPA's. Individuals using the established refuge trails will be allowed to use cross country skis and snowshoes for winter access. An outdoor education site is available for visitors to rest and have a lunch at while hiking the trails and enjoying area wildlife.

The CCP proposes to continue with the above uses and add the following to improve wildlife observation and wildlife photography opportunities along with access for all visitors.

- Repair flooded refuge roads for an auto tour or bicycle path (will only happen if flood waters recede)
- Construct a new photography blind
- Construct a boardwalk and observation deck
- Update and improve Complex Signs
- Establish a Coteau Birding Trail with sites located on the Refuge and WPA's
- Update existing brochures to new Service standards
- Pave with asphalt or concrete headquarter/visitor center and trail head parking lots

Availability of Resources:
Based on a review of the Complex budget allocated for this activity, there is adequate funding to ensure compatibility and to administer and manage the use at its current level. Additional funds will be required to provide additional programs and activities as outlined in the CCP.

Anticipated Impacts of Use:
Anticipated impacts from visitors engaged in wildlife observation and wildlife photography are minor damage to vegetation, littering, increased maintenance activity, potential conflicts with other visitors, and minor disturbances to wildlife. Because visitors are limited to the Complex Headquarters Island and on designated trails, wildlife observation and wildlife photography has only minor impacts on wildlife and does not detract from the primary purposes of the Refuge. All other potential impacts are considered minor.

Public Review and Comment:
This Compatibility Determination was distributed for public review and comment as an appendix to the draft Comprehensive Conservation Plan and Environmental Assessment for Waubay National Wildlife Refuge Complex.

Determination (Check one below):

_____ Use is Not Compatible

__X__ Use is Compatible With the Following Stipulations

Stipulations Necessary To Ensure Compatibility:
Public access for wildlife observation and wildlife photography will be limited to Refuge designated trails to assure minimal disturbance to wildlife and minimal conflict between user groups. Wildlife observation and wildlife photography activities will be reviewed annually to ensure this compatibility determination still applies.

Justification:
Based upon biological impacts described in the CCP and Environmental Assessment, it is determined that wildlife observation and wildlife photography within the Waubay National Wildlife Refuge Complex will not materially interfere with or detract from the purposes for which this Complex was established.

Secondly, wildlife observation and wildlife photography are priority public uses listed in the National Wildlife Refuge System Improvement Act. By facilitating these uses on the Complex, we will increase visitors' knowledge and appreciation of fish and wildlife, which will lead to increased public stewardship of wildlife and their habitats at the Complex and elsewhere. Increased public stewardship will support and complement the Service's actions in achieving the Refuge's purposes and the mission of the National Wildlife Refuge System.

Mandatory 10- or 15-year Re-evaluation Date: 2017

Use: Fishing

Description of Use:
The Refuge was opened to ice fishing in 1998 as rising water levels linked Hillebrand's and Spring Lakes (the main refuge lakes) and their associated peripheral marshes, to Waubay Lake. Suddenly, a world-class fishery for northern pike, walleye and yellow perch was thrust into Refuge lakes. Fishing is allowed from the close of Refuge rifle deer season (ice dependent) until ice-out in the spring. No motorized vehicles (passenger vehicles, snowmobiles, ATV's etc.) will be allowed to travel off existing trails and roads. The District WPA's are legally open to fishing as per their establishing legislation and the Federal Code of Regulations.

Availability of Resources:
Based on a review of the Complex budget allocated for this activity, there is adequate funding to ensure compatibility and to administer and manage the use at its current level. A RONS project for additional funds will provide increased law enforcement presence.

Anticipated Impacts of the Use:
Nearly all migratory birds and waterfowl have migrated from the Complex by the end of deer rifle season (December 1 or later). Remaining wildlife after this date concentrate their use on upland habitats, not frozen lakes. Harvests are regulated by South Dakota Game, Fish and Parks to take only surplus specimens, thus assuring viable, healthy populations within management and habitat guidelines. Restrictions to the fishing program assure that these activities have no adverse impacts on other wildlife species and little adverse impact on other public use programs.

Public Review and Comment:
This Compatibility Determination was distributed for public review and comment as an appendix to the draft Comprehensive Conservation Plan and Environmental Assessment for Waubay National Wildlife Refuge Complex.

Determination (Check one below):

_____ Use is Not Compatible

__X__ Use is Compatible With the Following Stipulations

Stipulations Necessary to Ensure Compatibility:
To ensure compatibility with National Wildlife Refuge System and Waubay Complex goals and objectives, movement of vehicles will be restricted to existing roads and trails to minimize disturbance to a wintering white-tailed deer herd. No ice-fishing prior to the end of rifle deer season will be allowed to avoid conflicts between deer hunters and ice-fisherman. Deer hunting was permitted for many years before the establishment of a fishing program. There are safety considerations to permitting two groups, one using high powered rifles, to utilize a relatively small area. Ice houses will be limited to day-use-only. Disturbance to Complex wildlife should be very minimal, with the above constraints.

Justification:
Based upon biological impacts described in the CCP and Environmental Assessment, it is determined that ice fishing within the Waubay National Wildlife Refuge Complex will not materially interfere with or detract from the purposes for which this Complex was established.

Secondly, fishing is a priority public use listed in the National Wildlife Refuge System Improvement Act. By facilitating this use on the Complex, we will increase visitors' knowledge and appreciation of fish and wildlife, which will lead to increased public stewardship of wildlife and their habitats at the Complex and in elsewhere. Increased public stewardship will support and complement the Service's actions in achieving the Refuge's purposes and the mission of the National Wildlife Refuge System.

Mandatory 10- or 15-year Re-evaluation Date: 2017

Use: Hunting

Description of Use:
Deer hunting may occur throughout the Refuge except for Headquarters Island which is closed to all hunting. There are currently three types of Refuge deer hunts, they include archery, muzzleloader and rifle seasons. Archery season is open to all properly licensed participants and muzzleloader and rifle seasons are by state permit only. Hunters are allowed to access island hunting areas with watercraft using only oars or paddles (no motorized watercraft are allowed, including electric motors). Hunting seasons begin in September with archery season and muzzleloader, and rifle seasons occur during November and early December. Archery season closes the end of December on the Refuge. The Wetland Management District WPA's are legally open to hunting as per their establishing legislation and the Federal Code of Regulations. The CCP does not propose any additional improvements beyond maintaining the existing use on WPA's.

Availability of Resources:
Based on a review of the Complex budget allocated for this activity, there is adequate funding to ensure compatibility and to administer and manage the use at its current level. A RONS project for additional funds will provide increased law enforcement presence.

Anticipated Impacts of Use:
Continuing this activity has shown no assessable environmental impact to the Refuge, its habitats, or wildlife species. With restrictions to hunting on Headquarters Island little disturbance will occur between hunting activities and all other allowable Refuge uses. With the use of non-motorized watercraft for island access, little disturbance will occur with migrating waterfowl and other migratory birds. Disturbance to wildlife is limited to occasional flushing of non-target species and the harvest of individual members of the species open to the hunting season in the periphery areas only. Restrictions to the hunting program assure that these activities have no adverse impacts on other wildlife species and little adverse impact to other public use programs. These activities are compliant with the purpose of the Refuge and the National Wildlife Refuge System Mission. Operating this activity does not alter the Refuge's ability to meet habitat goals, provides for the safety of local citizens, and supports several of the primary objectives of the Refuge.

Public Review and Comment:
This Compatibility Determination was distributed for public review and comment as an appendix to the draft Comprehensive Conservation Plan and Environmental Assessment for Waubay National Wildlife Refuge Complex.

Determination (check one below):

_____Use is Not Compatible

__X_ Use is Compatible With the Following Stipulations

Stipulations Necessary to Ensure Compatibility:
To ensure compatibility with National Wildlife Refuge System and Waubay Complex goals and objectives this activity can only occur under the following stipulations:
- No hunting will be permitted on Headquarters Island to prevent conflicts between other permitted activities and for safety of the visiting public.
- Only non-motorized watercraft (including electric motors) will be permitted on Refuge waters for use of transportation to and from Refuge Islands.
- Annually review all hunting activities and operations to ensure compliance with all applicable laws, regulations and policies.
- Annual population censuses will be completed to ensure population reduction is necessary to maintain deer numbers within the carrying capacity of the habitat.

Justification:
Based upon biological impacts described in the CCP and Environmental Assessment, it is determined that hunting within the Waubay National Wildlife Refuge Complex will not materially interfere with or detract from the purposes for which this Complex was established. In addition, deer hunting is necessary to meet the Refuge's habitat objectives and prevent adverse impacts to other wildlife species.

Secondly, hunting is a priority public use listed in the National Wildlife Refuge System Improvement Act. By facilitating this use on the Complex, we will increase visitors' knowledge and appreciation of fish and wildlife, which will lead to increased public stewardship of wildlife and their habitats at the Complex and elsewhere. Increased public stewardship will support and complement the Service's actions in achieving the Refuge's purposes and the mission of the National Wildlife Refuge System.

Mandatory 10- or 15-year Re-evaluation Date: 2017

Use: Trapping

Description of Use:
Provide for recreational trapping on Waubay Complex lands along with spring predator trapping to improve upland nesting bird success on the Complex. The Wetland Management District WPA's are legally open to trapping according to State regulations as per their establishing legislation and the Federal Code of Regulations.

Availability of resources:
Currently there is insufficient funding and staffing to manage the recreational trapping and spring predator trapping on the Complex. The Complex recreational trapping program will be enhanced through additional law enforcement staff. To administer a spring predator trapping program additional biological staff for monitoring of predator populations and upland bird production will be required. Both positions are listed in the RONS Appendix N.

Anticipated Impacts of the Use:
Trapping removes individual animals from wildlife populations, and predator populations are temporarily reduced up to and during the nesting season. Spring predator trapping increases nesting success of upland nesting birds. There would be direct mortality of target animals, some vegetation trampling by personnel, and some minor increase in general wildlife disturbance in trapping areas due to human and vehicular traffic. There is the possibility of injury to nonmarket wildlife that are caught in traps such as badgers, weasels, an occasional rabbit, domestic dogs and feral cats.

Public Review and Comment:
This Compatibility Determination was distributed for public review and comment as an appendix to the draft Comprehensive Conservation Plan and Environmental Assessment for Waubay National Wildlife Refuge Complex.

Determination (check one below):

_____Use is Not Compatible

___X___Use is Compatible With the Following Stipulations

Stipulations Necessary to Ensure Compatibility:
- Trapping will be conducted in a manner that will remove only targeted species or species removed for public health and safety concerns.
- Recreational trapping will occur within regular State seasons and will not conflict with other public uses.
- Trapping for predators outside of regular season will be coordinated with the South Dakota Game, Fish and Parks.
- Detailed trapping records will be maintained for refuge and staff trappers.
- No trapping will take place in areas of high public use areas, especially Headquarters Island unless done for health and safety reasons.
- No exposed bait will be placed near traps that might attract eagles or other raptors.
- Traps must be monitored at a minimum of every 24 hours.
- Monitoring of nest success in areas targeted for predator removal to determine effectiveness and need for next year's trapping (only when nest success falls below 30 percent Mayfield will trapping be conducted).

Justification:
Recreational trapping removes excessive wildlife populations and provides public recreational opportunity. Spring predator trapping will benefit upland nesting birds, including many species of waterfowl, when predator populations are reduced during the nesting season. Long-term negative effects to these predator populations will not take place as conducted trapping activities cannot feasibly remove enough animals to permanently impact these populations.

Mandatory 10- or 15-year Re-evaluation Date: 2017

Use: Farming, Grazing and Haying

Description of Proposed Use:
Continue upland management activities such as farming, grazing and haying that are conducted under permit by private individuals. Currently, these economic uses are used as management tools to manage habitat for wildlife. Farming averages 100 acres each year in the Complex, including Refuge fields and grassland restoration activities on WPA's. Cattle grazing is currently used as a management tool throughout the Complex and averages 2,000 acres a year. Haying is used on the Refuge and District to improve grassland conditions and control invasive weed species with an average of 200 acres hayed annually. The CCP proposes to maintain the number of crop acres, and may include increasing grazing and haying if these tools are required for improving habitat.

Availability of Resources:
Current resources are stretched thin to maintain existing programs. If additional staff support were available, these programs could be expanded to utilize these tools more effectively and monitoring could be accomplished. Additional management and biological staff are identified in the RONS Appendix N. These positions will be necessary to fully accomplish the goals of the CCP and improve the existing programs.

Anticipated Impacts of the Use:
Current management affects less than 5 percent of the upland habitat annually. This management is not evenly distributed over the entire Complex, and the percentage of upland receiving optimum management is considered to be much less than 5 percent. General habitat conditions on the Complex would gradually deteriorate due to long periods of non-prescribed rest. While some wildlife disturbance does occur with these activities, the benefits to wildlife far out-weigh these disturbances. No cultural resources would be impacted. No impact to endangered species should occur; however, habitat suitability for the Dakota skipper and regal fritillary would continue to deteriorate without some form of defoliation treatment.

Public Review and Comment:
This Compatibility Determination was distributed for public review and comment as an appendix to the draft Comprehensive Conservation Plan and Environmental Assessment for Waubay National Wildlife Refuge Complex.

Determination (check one below):

_____Use is Not Compatible

___X__ Use is Compatible With the Following Stipulations

Stipulations Necessary to Ensure Compatibility:
- General and special conditions are required for each permit to ensure consistency with management objectives.
- Farming permittees are restricted to a list of approved chemicals which are less detrimental to wildlife, use of only the necessary amount to control problem spots, and to report their use yearly.
- Farming permittees must leave a portion of the crop for wildlife use.
- Cattle grazing permittees are required to follow a short-term rotational grazing system to provide appropriate stimulation of grasses.
- Grazing permittees must comply with State Livestock Health Laws.
- Haying will be restricted to after July 15 to avoid disturbance to nesting birds.
- Haying permittees are required to report and mow noxious weeds in their areas.

Justification:
Without these uses there would be many adverse reactions. Upland habitat conditions would deteriorate without the use of a full range of upland management tools. Exotic and noxious weed species would increase and habitat diversity would decrease causing a decline in wildlife diversity. Migratory bird production and diversity would decrease as habitat suitability for these species declined. Consumptive and non-consumptive wildlife-oriented recreational opportunities would decline as wildlife diversity and populations decreased. Although the prescribed management techniques listed in the proposed use are not adequate in scope to prevent such declines from taking place in all upland habitat sites, the limited upland management which does take place will diversify and improve treated grasslands.

Mandatory 10- or 15-year Re-evaluation Date: 2017

Use: Research

Description of Use:
The Waubay Complex receives periodic requests to conduct scientific research. Priority would be given to studies that support the Complex purposes, goals and objectives. This would include, for example, studies that contribute to the enhancement, protection, use, preservation and management of native Complex wildlife populations and their habitats, and would also include cultural resources. Research applicants must submit a proposal that would outline: 1) objectives of the study; 2) justification for the study; 3) detailed methodology and schedule; 4) potential impacts on Complex wildlife and/or habitat, including disturbance (short- and long-term), injury, or mortality; 5) personnel required; 6) costs to the Complex, if any; and 7) end products (i.e. reports, publications). Research proposals would be reviewed by Complex staff, Regional Office Branch of Refuge Biology and others, as appropriate. Evaluation criteria will include, but not be limited to, the following:

1) Research that will contribute to priority management activities will have higher priority than other requests.

2) Research that will conflict with higher priority research, monitoring or management programs may not be granted.

3) Research projects that can be done elsewhere off-Waubay Complex lands, are less likely to be approved.

4) Research which causes undue disturbance or is intrusive, will likely not be granted. Level and type of disturbance will be carefully weighed when evaluating a request.

5) Research evaluation will determine if any effort has been made to minimize disturbance through study design, including considering adjusting location, timing, scope, number of permittees, study methods, number of study sites, etc.

6) If staffing or logistics make it impossible for the Complex to monitor researcher activity this may be reason to deny the request depending on the circumstances.

7) The length of the project will be considered and agreed upon before approval. Projects will not be open ended, and at a minimum, will be reviewed annually.

Availability of Resources:
Direct costs to administer research activities are primarily in the form of staff time and transportation. It is estimated that current staff is adequate to manage small and short-term research projects. RONS projects for additional biological and management staff will be required to monitor complex and long-term research activities. Proposals will only be accepted if funding and personnel are available to adequately monitor all research activities.

Anticipated Impacts of Use:
Minimal impact to Complex wildlife and habitats will be expected with research studies. Some level of disturbance is expected with all research activities since most researchers will be entering areas that are normally closed to the public and may be collecting samples or handling wildlife. Special Use Permit conditions will include special conditions to ensure that impact to wildlife and habitats are kept to a minimum.

Public Review and Comment:
This Compatibility Determination was distributed for public review and comment as an appendix to the draft Comprehensive Conservation Plan and Environmental Assessment for Waubay National Wildlife Refuge Complex.

Determination:

_____ Use is not Compatible

__X__ Use is Compatible with the Following Stipulations

Stipulations Necessary to Ensure Compatibility:
- If the proposed research methods would impact or potentially impact Complex resources (habitat or wildlife), it must be demonstrated that the research is necessary (i.e. critical to survival of a species, will enhance restoration activities of native species, will help in control of invasive species or provide valuable information that will guide future Refuge or Service activities), and the researcher must identify the issues in advance of the impact.
- Highly intrusive or manipulative research is generally not permitted in order to protect native wildlife populations and habitats in which they live.
- Research that doesn't involve birds will be conducted outside of the breeding season of avian species in all possible circumstances.
- Project Leader can suspend/modify conditions/terminate on-refuge research that is already permitted and in progress, should unacceptable impacts or issues arise or be noted.

Justification:
Research projects will contribute to the enhancement, protection, use, preservation, and management of native Complex wildlife populations and their habitats. In view of the potential impacts associated research activities can have on the U.S. Fish & Wildlife Service's ability to achieve Complex purposes, sufficient restrictions would be placed on the researcher to ensure that disturbance is kept to a minimum. This program as described is determined to be compatible.

Mandatory 10- or 15-year Re-evaluation Date: 2017

Waubay Complex Compatibility Determinations Approval

Refuge Manager/
Project Leader
Approval: _____   23 Aug. 2002
                    (Signature)   (Date)

Concurrence:

Refuge Supervisor: _____   8/29/02
                       (Signature)   (Date)

Regional Chief,
National Wildlife
Refuge System: _____   8/30/02
                    (Signature)   (Date)

Appendix M. Plans and Organizations Affecting Waubay Complex

North American Waterfowl Management Plan - an international strategy that coordinates the efforts of public and private conservation groups to protect, restore and enhance wetland habitats for declining waterfowl populations. Implementation occurs regionally, within one of nine habitat joint ventures in the U.S. Waubay Complex falls under the scope of the Prairie Pothole Joint Venture, which works to promote waterfowl conservation and the preservation of all wetland and associated-upland species in the Prairie Pothole Region of the U.S. and Canada.

The Nature Conservancy - the world's leading private international conservation group dedicated to preserving the plants, animals, and natural communities that represent the diversity of life on Earth. The Tallgrass Prairie Ecoregional Plan works to ensure the long-term survival of the remaining tallgrass prairie that occurs within this ecoregion, which is considered to be less than 4 percent of its historical range.

Partners in Flight - a cooperative effort among individuals, government agencies, and nongovernmental organizations to address the growing concerns about declines in populations of many land bird species, especially those not covered by existing conservation initiatives. Efforts focus on improving monitoring and inventory, research, management, and education programs involving birds and their habitats.

Partners for Fish and Wildlife - Helps accomplish the mission of the U.S. Fish & Wildlife Service by offering technical and financial assistance to private landowners to voluntarily restore wetlands and other fish and wildlife habitats on their land. Emphasizes reestablishment of native vegetation and ecological communities for the benefit of wildlife in concert with the needs and desires of private landowners.

South Dakota Natural Heritage Program - a cooperative project between South Dakota Game, Fish and Parks and The Nature Conservancy to monitor and protect rare and endangered species or unique features and document potential threats to the continued survival of such species or communities in the State of South Dakota.

Western Hemisphere Shorebird Reserve Network - a joint program of Manomet Observatory and Wetlands International that focuses on the study, management, and protection of wetlands and grasslands essential for migratory shorebirds.

Dakota Tallgrass Prairie Wildlife Management Area - a grassland easement program developed by the USFWS to preserve 190,000 acres of native tallgrass prairie in eastern North and South Dakota.

U.S. Department of Agriculture, Natural Resources Conservation Service - has several programs aimed at conserving tallgrass prairie rangeland and protecting highly erodible soils while providing wildlife habitat. The Environmental Quality Incentives Program (EQIP) provides ranchers and farmers with information on grazing systems, water development, and educational programs. The Conservation Reserve Program (CRP) allows highly erodible croplands to be set-aside and planted to a mixture of native grasses for 10 to 15 year contracts. The Wildlife Habitat Incentive Program (WHIP) provides expertise and funding for planting native grasses.

Ducks Unlimited - a private organization whose mission is to fulfill the annual life cycle needs of North American waterfowl by protecting, enhancing, restoring, and managing important wetlands and associated uplands. They are initializing a Revolving Land Acquisition Program on the Prairie Coteau of northeastern South Dakota that is aimed at restoration of waterfowl habitat on large tracts.

Friends of Prairie - a group of private citizens focused on raising public awareness and support of issues related to the conservation and preservation of tallgrass prairie in the Dakotas.

		RONS Projects Waubay National Wildlife Refuge and Waubay Wetland Management District			
Priority No.	*Links to CCP Goal*	*Project Description*	*First Year Need*	*Recurring Annual Need*	*FTE*
1	R1, R3, R4, D1, D3, D4	Initiate environmental education program - Education Specialist	$128,000	$63,000	1.0
2	R1, D1	Restore 500 acres of tallgrass grasslands - Maintenance Worker	$164,000	$99,000	1.0
3	R1, D1	Improve noxious weed control on 500 acres of native prairie - Maintenance Worker	$144,000	$79,000	1.0
4	R1, R2, R3, R4, D1, D2, D3, D4	Protect 20,000 acres of prairie wetlands and grasslands - Administrative Clerk	$118,000	$53,000	1.0
5	R1, R2, R3, R4, D1, D2, D3, D4	Protect 10,000 acres of threatened grassland and wetland habitats - Resource Specialist	$139,000	$74,000	1.0
6	R1, R2, R3, R4, D1, D2, D3, D4	Develop a GIS based habitat mapping system for 250,000 acres of Refuge System lands	$93,000		
7	R3, R4, D3, D4	Improve enforcement of wetland and grassland easements on 200,000 acres - Law Enforcement Officer	$139,000	$74,000	1.0
8	R1, R2, R4, D1, D2, D4	Survey bird and plant communities - Biologist	$128,000	$63,000	1.0
9	R1, D1	Improve 2,000 acres of grassland on waterfowl production area - Maintenance Worker	$152,000	$87,000	1.0
10	R1, R3, R4, D1, D3, D4	Increase management intensity of Refuge System lands - Manager	$76,000	$37,000	0.5
11	R1, R3, R4, D1, D3, D4	Expand land management activities - Manager	$166,000	$101,000	1.0
12	R1, R2, R4, D1, D2, D4	Survey plant communities on 200 waterfowl production areas - Bio Tech	$277,000	$77,000	1.0
Totals			$1,724,000	$807,000	10.5

Appendix O. MMS List

	MMS Projects Waubay National Wildlife Refuge and Waubay Wetland Management District		
Priority No.	**Links to CCP Goal**	**Project Description**	**Estimated Cost**
1	R1, R2, R3, R4, D1, D2, D3, D4	Repair Office/Visitor Center heating and cooling	$27,000
2	R1, R2, R3, R4, D1, D2, D3, D4	Replace WPA boundary fence	$79,000
3	R1, R2, R3, R4, D1, D2, D3, D4	Replace WPA boundary signs	$65,000
4	R1, R2, D1, D2,	Replace 1978 implement truck	$55,000
5	R1, R2, R3, R4, D1, D2, D3, D4	Stablize Office/Visitor Center lakeshore	$105,000
6	R1, R2, D1, D2	Replace 1979 farm tractor	$96,000
7	R1, R2, D1, D2	Replace 1979 tandem disc	$25,000
8	R1, R2, R3, R4, D1, D2, D3, D4	Replace WPA boundary fence	$79,000
9	R1, R2, R3, R4, D1, D2, D3, D4	Replace WPA boundary fence	$65,000
10	R1, R2, D1, D2	Replace 1980 skid loader	$48,000
11	R1, R2, R3, R4, D1, D2, D3, D4	Replace WPA boundary fence	$79,000
12	R1, R2, D1, D2	Replace 1984 implement trailer	$25,000
Totals			$748,000

Appendix P. List of Preparers

Waubay NWR Staff:
Laura Hubers, Wildlife Biologist
Jarrod Lee, Refuge Operations Specialist
Doug Leschisin, Deputy Project Leader
Larry Martin, Project Leader
Connie Mueller, Refuge Operations Specialist

USFWS, Division of Planning, Denver, CO
Bridget McCann, Wildlife Biologist, Team Leader
Toni Griffin, Landscape Architect, Team Leader
Sean Fields, GIS Coordinator, Mapping
Barbara Shupe, Writer/Editor, Document Layout

Appendix Q. Public Involvement / Response to Comments

Various methods were used to involve the public in this planning process. Three public meetings and open houses were held at the beginning of the planning process. Sixteen hundred questionnaires were distributed to all township, county, state and Federal elected officials, past permit holders (easement and special use), anyone who entered into a new easement contract in the last 10 years, all private lands cooperators, organizations that the Refuge deals with, and Refuge deer hunters. The questionnaires were distributed to gather ideas and suggestions on issues the public believed should be addressed at Waubay Complex. A 7 percent returned response rate resulted in a mix of suggestions, as well as some issues that are not under Waubay Complex jurisdiction. Information was also distributed through a web site and newsletter updates. A mailing list was complied of all persons that commented or requested notification (Appendix G). Lastly, the Draft Plan was distributed for comment to everyone on the mailing list.

This section will generally list the types of comments received during the process, whether written or verbal, and provide the Service's response to each. No attempt was made to quantify the number of people making each comment.

There was an overall agreement among respondents that they are glad the Refuge system is here to provide free access to land for relaxation, education, hunting and fishing opportunities, and a place for wildlife and habitat. Whether people use the land or not, the knowledge that the land is here was satisfying to most.

Habitat

Comments:
✓ Do not change management priority of Refuge or WMD
✓ Need more active habitat management on WMD
✓ Manage Refuge habitats for native wildlife only
✓ Allow buffalo grazing on Refuge lands
✓ Too much haying and grazing on Federal lands
Response: Traditionally, the most common management technique used in the Waubay Complex has been cattle grazing, with lesser treatments of prescribed burning or haying. Prairie ecosystems evolved with frequent disturbances by grazing animals (buffalo, elk) and fire. These disturbances evolved with native wildlife and are compatible. Plans are to maintain grasslands and wetlands in quality condition for wildlife using more frequent management treatments than has been used in the past. Buffalo ranching is becoming more common in the area, and with the necessary fencing, is another option for treating grasslands. In order to provide quality habitat, haying, grazing or burning generally need to be used every 3 to 5 years.

Comments:
✓ Encourage biological methods for weed control
✓ Increase weed control on Refuge lands
✓ Decrease amount of chemical weed control - increase non-chemical methods
Response: The Service's active involvement in biological control insects have significantly reduced leafy spurge on several Waterfowl Production Areas and adjacent private, tribal, and state lands. Noxious weeds negatively impact native grasslands and the wildlife using them. The Service is committed to reducing noxious weeds (Canada thistle, leafy spurge, and others) using biological, mechanical, and cultural controls.

Comments:
✓ Need grassland buffer around easement, WPA and Refuge lands to filter agricultural impacts
✓ Emphasize watershed management planning
Response: Payments are made to landowners for wetland easement contracts to protect wetlands from draining, burning, leveling, and filling: these contracts do not address grassland buffers adjacent to these wetlands. However, the Service's grassland easement program protects grasslands from conversion to other uses and indirectly protects wetlands from agricultural runoff. The Service's Partners for Wildlife Program has been very active working with watershed groups to improve watersheds.

Comment:
✓ Control water on easements to allow lowering water levels
Response: Service easement contracts are designed to protect wetlands in their natural state and do not permit artificial lowering of water levels.

Comments:
✓ Use boundary signs only - no fences
✓ Maintain fences
Response: Boundary fences serve several purposes including marking a clear boundary for adjacent landowners and visitors, discouraging vehicle trespass, and facilitating cattle grazing to treat grasslands. Plans are to maintain existing fences and erect new ones where necessary.

Comments:
✓ Increase tree plantings
✓ Remove trees from around WPA wetlands
✓ Plant more native shrubs on WPAs
Response: Trees are native to certain localities of the Complex, namely Waubay NWR, around some large lakes, and many drainages on the eastern face of the Prairie Coteau. The rest of the Complex had very few trees at time of European settlement, but plantings and fire suppression has increased trees greatly on the overall landscape. Plans are to increase plantings of native grasses, forbs, and shrubs to recreate more native plant communities. If more burns are conducted nonnative trees may be inevitably removed. Nonnative species will not be planted.

Comments:
- ✓ Plant crops on Refuge to reduce depredation on private land
- ✓ Reestablish Refuge island food plots when water levels drop
- ✓ No crops on Refuge, native species only

Response: The primary purpose of Refuge croplands is to provide food for wintering deer, especially in years of heavy snow. Presence of corn, alfalfa, and other crops takes browsing pressure off trees and shrubs when food resources are scarce in tough winters. Plans are to eliminate food plots on Refuge islands and restore forest communities in these locations, but maintain croplands on other sites.

Comments:
- ✓ Increase attention paid to rare plants and animals on Refuge
- ✓ Increase habitat management for butterflies
- ✓ Use native plants for reseeding, haying, and burning to improve grassland management

Response: Increased monitoring efforts should give the Service a better idea of what plant and wildlife resources are present on federal lands, including rare plants and animals. Plans are to increase emphasis on plantings of native grasses, forbs, and shrubs. Prescribed burning will be increased to enhance and maintain native vegetation.

Comments:
- ✓ Buy only drained wetlands and restore them
- ✓ Expand land acquisition program
- ✓ Expand easement acquisition
- ✓ Acquire fee-title and easements that are adjacent to current Refuge lands
- ✓ Step up land acquisition to take advantage of current conditions
- ✓ No new acquisition - manage current lands better
- ✓ Increase acquisition of native woodlands
- ✓ Establish easements only where public hunting will be allowed - make a condition of the easement
- ✓ Better explain to sellers the terms of easement contracts; provide guidelines on exactly what can and can't be done on easement lands.

Response: Fee-title acquisition of Waterfowl Productions Areas began in the Complex in 1959, but few purchases have taken place since the mid-1980s, when increase emphasis was placed on acquisition of wetland and grassland easements. Service acquisition of rights to privately owned wetlands and grasslands has been a popular program since the early 1960s, and continues to this day. Plans are to continue the priority of acquisition of high quality wetland and grassland easements on privately owned lands. All terms of easement contracts are fully explained at the time of sale. It is impossible to exactly define all permitted and non-permitted actions on easement lands as proposed uses by landowners are not foreseeable into perpetuity. Only broad guidelines, such as "no alteration of grasslands" is possible until specific uses are proposed. Decisions are then made based on contract terms and intent. There are no plans to change the terms of these easement contracts or requirements of wetland conditions. Current funding sources are for waterfowl production so acquisition of native woodlands will not be possible without additional funding sources.

Wildlife

Comment:
- ✓ Use artificial nest structures on all WPAs

Response: Mallards and Canada geese are the waterfowl species that most commonly use nest structures. The Service has de-emphasized the use of nest structures for geese because of concerns of over-population of this bird across its range. Past programs have partnered with conservation organizations to encourage nest structures for mallards. Plans are to continue with this effort.

Comment:
- ✓ Need predator control for fox, raccoon and skunk

Response: Many studies have shown that predators may impact nest success of ground nesting birds, including waterfowl, especially in areas where grassland habitat has been destroyed or fragmented. Predator management is most successful where it is undertaken on large blocks of land. Research by Delta Waterfowl Foundation in North Dakota has found that conducting predator removal on Township size blocks (36 square miles) has increased ground nesting bird success significantly. Currently, we have no predator removal programs in place within the Refuge or Wetland Management District, but would consider such actions where warranted.

Comment:
- ✓ Need sanctuaries on WPAs for resting waterfowl

Response: During negotiations in Congress for the Small Wetlands Program it was agreed that the WPAs would not be subjected to the "inviolate sanctuary" requirements of the Migratory Bird Conservation Act, which required that no more than 40 percent of a refuge could be opened for migratory bird hunting. In honor of that agreement, it was then codified in the Code of Federal Regulations that all WPAs would be opened to hunting.

Comment:
- ✓ Want an area for an elk herd

Response: The Service has no plans to introduce elk to the Refuge or Waterfowl Production Areas. There are no federally owned tracts of land large enough to maintain an elk herd.

Comment:
- ✓ Introduce the bald eagle to the Refuge

Response: Recent expansion of bald eagle populations has resulted in the national bird being downlisted from endangered to threatened. It is currently proposed for delisting altogether. At least three active bald eagle nests were recently established in the six county Waubay Wetland Management District, so it would not be surprising if eagles chose to use the Refuge as a nesting site. Plans do not call for establishing a hacking site, since there is no assurance those birds would return to the Refuge.

Comment:
- ✓ Control populations of cormorants and pelicans

Response: Double-crested cormorants and white pelicans are protected migratory birds listed by the Migratory Bird Treaty Act. Any efforts to control these populations would have to be undertaken on a nationwide scale, and is outside the scope of this local plan.

Comment:
- ✓ Maintain bluebird boxes at Refuge

Response: Plans are to maintain current levels of bluebird boxes on Waubay National Wildlife Refuge.

Comment:
✓ Assess impacts of bison grazing on Refuge cultural resource sites
Response: Plans include a more detailed cultural resource inventory of the Refuge. Impacts to any sites potentially disturbed by grazing, prescribed burning, or other management would have to be considered prior to undertaking management actions.

Comment:
✓ Encourage more snow goose use of Refuge
Response: Snow goose use of the Refuge has traditionally been very low, especially in the fall. Most falls have no sightings of snow geese resting on the Refuge. The main flyway of snow geese, in South Dakota, is 50-miles or more to the west. Efforts to attract resting snow geese are likely to fail.

Public Use
Comments:
✓ Restrict Refuge deer hunting to muzzleloader and archery
✓ Allow non-motorized boat access for deer hunting
✓ Decrease number of deer tags on Refuge
✓ Survey deer hunters before implementing restrictions
Response: Past Refuge deer hunting opportunities included archery hunting as part of South Dakota's general archery deer seasons and lottery hunts for muzzleloader and firearm deer hunts. Allowing all three types of hunts enables a larger group of people to experience this unique eastern South Dakota hunt. Rifle hunters are more effective at providing overpopulation solutions for the Refuge. Numbers of lottery tags for Refuge hunts are determined annually by the Service and South Dakota Game, Fish and Parks Department. License numbers are based on past season hunting success, winter survival, herd size, and the desire to maintain a quality, uncrowded hunting experience. Hunters are surveyed annually with the Refuge routinely receiving high marks for its deer hunting program. Planned restrictions on hunter densities are based on hunter feedback and safety concerns. Non-motorized boat access has been allowed for deer hunters desiring to hunt Refuge islands. Plans are to maintain similar strategies for Refuge deer hunts.

Comment:
✓ Consider offering pheasant hunting on appropriate upland areas of the Refuge.
Response: Waubay NWR, and the immediate surrounding area, is marginal pheasant habitat. In 2002, less than a dozen pheasants were found on the Refuge. There are considerable pheasant hunting opportunities in the region. However, if pheasant numbers increase, which could warrant pheasant hunting, consideration would be given to opening the Refuge to pheasant hunting.

Comments:
✓ Restrict fishing by time or location to protect wildlife
✓ Open Refuge to roadside fishing all year, all Refuge for ice fishing
✓ Open Refuge lakes to non-motorized boats
✓ Develop a boat landing on Refuge
✓ Improve access for ice fishing - more road access or shuttle
✓ Make full use of fishing resource
✓ Expand youth hunting and fishing programs
✓ Need ice fishing regulations/information at Spring Lake overlook
Response: Sport fishing became possible in 1997, for the first time in the Refuge's history, when the expanding waters of the Waubay Lake Chain joined with Refuge lakes. Fishing is a priority public use on Refuges, if it is compatible with Refuge purposes, namely "a refuge and breeding ground for migratory birds and other wildlife." The Service determined that open water boating and fishing activities would interfere with breeding and resting migratory birds. Limited ice-fishing was allowed since most migratory birds and a large wintering deer herd would not be disturbed by this public use. Restrictions placed on ice-fishing included no vehicles on the ice (including shuttle vehicles), no over-night shacks, and no night fishing to allow the wintering deer herd undisturbed access to their feeding sites. These restrictions allow both fishing and wildlife protection. Year-round roadside/shoreline fishing will not be allowed for several reasons: safety concerns, road damage during wet conditions, and lack of adequate parking areas. Youth fishing programs and increased information disbursal are being pursued.

Comment:
✓ Develop fishery (stocking) and provide access on large WPAs
Response: The primary purpose of Waterfowl Production Areas is to provide habitat for the production of waterfowl. Several studies have shown that ducklings and fish compete for the same invertebrate food source, so stocking of fish may lower a wetland's capability to produce ducklings and other water birds. For this reason, plans do not include developing fisheries on WPAs.

Comments:
✓ Additional road access to Westwoods Island (Refuge)
✓ Continue public access to Refuge, WMD
✓ Improve road and trail access to Refuge lands
✓ Improve access for elderly and disabled on Refuge and WPAs
✓ Decrease Refuge road access except for disabled
✓ Allow access to trails for wildlife watching on WPAs
✓ Don't allow vehicles on WPAs
Response: Much of the Refuge's traditional road system was inundated by rising waters of the Waubay Lake system. Costs to raise these flooded roads would be astronomical and degrade the water quality of the entire system by dumping tons of suspended solids into the water. Refuge facilities have been retrofitted to allow access for visitors with disabilities and new universally accessible trails will provide further opportunities. Vehicle access is limited to existing public roads on all Complex lands to limit damage to vegetation and disturbance to wildlife. The Service does not have jurisdiction on these public roads and their upkeep. Wildlife observation, by foot, is permitted on some Refuge trails and Waterfowl Production Areas.

Comments:
- ✓ Promote a tribal/Refuge tourism cooperative program
- ✓ Increase public relations with sportsmen groups to improve image and public participation
- ✓ Expand public "work days" - volunteer projects beyond those for youth groups
- ✓ Create citizen committee to provide advice for Refuge management

Response: Increased public input and volunteerism are important cornerstones of the 1997 Refuge Improvement Act and plans call for an increase of both in the Waubay Complex. Feasible cooperative programs that result will be pursued.

Comments:
- ✓ Need more interpretation about different wildlife habitats
- ✓ Provide more wildlife educational opportunities - spring bird walks, etc.
- ✓ Extend weekend hours for visitor center
- ✓ Formalize and enhance relationship with NE-SO-DAK
- ✓ Limit amount of visitation on Refuge to protect wildlife

Response: Plans include more wildlife compatible interpretation and educational opportunities for the public within the Waubay Complex. These opportunities may include a variety of avenues.

Comments:
- ✓ Provide primitive tent camping on Refuge
- ✓ Want horseback riding, hiking, overnight camping on Refuge
- ✓ Allow mountain biking on Refuge lands
- ✓ Keep picnic area available

Response: Camping is available on nearby State parks, but is not a permitted use on the Refuge. Horseback riding and mountain biking is permitted on existing public roads, but not off-road on federal lands. These restrictions are in place to limit damage to vegetation and disturbance to wildlife and make activities wildlife compatible. The Refuge picnic area serves as a focal point for environmental education programs and plans are to continue this use as water levels permit.

Comment:
- ✓ Complete thorough archaeological survey for all Refuge and WMD lands

Response: Plans are to complete more archaeological surveys in areas suspected of having these resources.

Private Lands

Comments:
- ✓ Provide nest structures for private lands
- ✓ Create more wetlands on private lands
- ✓ Create 10-year management contracts for private lands - short-term easements
- ✓ Need more incentives for private landowners to improve water quality
- ✓ Subsidize native grass seed purchases for private landowners
- ✓ Expand private lands program efforts in Upper Big Sioux watershed
- ✓ Subsidize seeding on Conservation Reserve Program lands
- ✓ More outreach about pasture management on private lands

Response: Partners for Wildlife programs are funded through partnerships with federal agencies, state agencies, conservation organizations, and private landowners. Most of the above programs have been funded through Partners for Wildlife in the past and are likely to be funded in the future, if partners remain interested and funding resources remain steady.

Issues under Authority of Other Agencies/Groups

Comments:
- ✓ Stock fish in Refuge and private lands
- ✓ Provide boat ramps and public use facilities on Waubay Lake
- ✓ Increase pheasant population
- ✓ Make more deer tags available for Refuge and WPAs
- ✓ Landowners should have authority to control wildlife depredation on their own land
- ✓ Provide or acquire walk-in rights on private lands

Response: These programs or activities are the responsibility of the South Dakota Game, Fish and Parks Department and are beyond the scope of this plan.

Comments:
- ✓ Change high water mark for area lakes
- ✓ Lower level of Waubay Lake
- ✓ Eliminate all drainage onto public lands

Response: These programs or activities are the responsibility of the South Dakota Department of Environment and Natural Resources and are beyond the scope of this plan.

Comment:
- ✓ Refuge should pay 100 percent of property tax due on Federal lands

Response: Federal agencies, such as the U.S. Fish & Wildlife Service, by law, do not pay property taxes, but make a payment-in-lieu-of-taxes to counties every year. Payments are appropriated annually by the Congress of the United States and are beyond the scope of this plan.

Comments:
- ✓ Allow more haying and grazing on Conservation Reserve Program lands
- ✓ Reestablish the Waterbank program
- ✓ Need weed and gopher control on Conservation Reserve Program lands

Response: These programs or activities are the responsibility of the Farm Service Agency of the U.S. Department of Agriculture and are beyond the scope of this plan.

Waubay National Wildlife Refuge Complex
44401 134A Street
Waubay, South Dakota 57273-5301
605 / 947 4521
email: waubay@fws.gov
http://waubay.fws.gov/

For Relay Service Connection
TTY/Voice: 711

U. S. Fish & Wildlife Service
http://www.fws.gov
http://mountain-prairie.fws.gov/planning

For Refuge Information
1 800 / 344 WILD

September 2002

Cover Photo USFWS